Going to University from Care

Sonia Jackson, Sarah Ajayi and Margaret Quigley

First published in 2005 by the Institute of Education, University of London,
20 Bedford Way, London WC1H 0AL
www.ioe.ac.uk/publications

Over 100 years of excellence in education

British Library Cataloguing in Publication Data:
A catalogue record for this publication is available from the British Library

ISBN 0 85473 715 4

Cover design by Tim McPhee
Page make-up by Ward Partnership, Saffron Walden

Production services by
Book Production Consultants plc, Cambridge

Printed by Cromwell Press, Trowbridge, Wiltshire

Contents

Key words   care leavers; higher education; resilience; unaccompanied asylum seekers; university access; widening participation

Foreword

by the Rt Hon Ruth Kelly MP

SECRETARY OF STATE FOR EDUCATION AND SKILLS

I was very pleased to be asked to write the foreword to the final report of the *By Degrees* research team. As the first ever research about how care leavers experience university, this work makes a significant contribution to developing policy on widening access to higher education and on improving the support provided to young people in and leaving care. Both these issues are a priority for my Department.

Every reasonable parent wants to do all they can to unlock their child's potential. Directors of children's services and lead members for children's services will need to take personal responsibility on behalf of their authority for improving the support that they offer to looked-after children. The responsibility does not end as the young people leave care but continues as they begin to find their own pathway into adulthood.

Young people in local authority care are a particularly vulnerable group. Those who gain a place at university have already accomplished a remarkable achievement, and the report highlights the barriers they have to overcome. It also includes powerful messages for local authorities and their partners about the importance of recognising the needs of young people so that they can receive the reliable and consistent practical and emotional support that will be necessary to enable them to succeed in their studies. Local authorities and other agencies responsible for providing services to care leavers should take note of the report's findings as part of their drive to become excellent corporate parents to the children in and leaving their care.

Acknowledgements

An action research project such as this one depends for its success on the cooperation of many people and organisations. The authors would like to thank all those who have helped to bring it to a successful conclusion, in particular:

The Trustees of the Frank Buttle Trust, who commissioned the research and raised the funds to carry it out. We also thank the Department for Education and Skills and the charitable bodies that contributed funds: Calouste Gulbenkian Foundation UK, the Esmée Fairbairn Foundation, Freemasons' Grand Charity, Garfield Weston Foundation and the Pilgrim Trust. Special thanks to the KPMG Foundation, which in addition to contributing funds to the research project, also funded the dissemination programme.

The project owes a great deal to Hugo Perks, former Director of the Frank Buttle Trust, whose vision turned a tentative idea into a reality. Hugo helped to develop the proposal, thought of the name *By Degrees*, steered the work through its first three years and made a substantial contribution to the interim report, published in 2003. Gerri McAndrew, Chief Executive, Karen Melton, Christine Manning-Prior and all the staff of the Frank Buttle Trust have continued to provide much appreciated support, advice and encouragement over the course of the project. However, responsibility for this report and the views expressed in it remain with the authors.

Simon Richey, Education Director of the Calouste Gulbenkian Foundation UK, has taken a keen interest in this project from its inception and the Foundation funded the preliminary study which showed that the proposed research was needed and feasible.

The idea for the project originated in a discussion with Dr Peter McParlin, who has used his personal and professional experience to campaign tirelessly for young people in care to have the same opportunity as others to go to university and to pursue their education as far as their aspirations and ability can take them.

We thank our Advisory Group, chaired by Sir William Utting, for consistently valuable advice and support. Their strongly expressed view that the findings of the research should be widely known inspired us to seek further funding for the dissemination programme. Susanna Cheal and Helen Hibbert of The Who Cares? Trust have provided much useful information and continue to work with us to ensure that our findings reach as many professionals and young people as possible.

Our colleagues at the Thomas Coram Research Unit have provided an invaluable reference group in addition to giving us much practical help with research methods. We thank in particular Peter Aggleton, Peter Moss, Charlie Owen, Antonia Simon, Steff Hazlehurst and Jethro Perkins.

Eleven local authorities have acted as an ongoing sounding board throughout the project. We thank them and all those who responded to our two postal surveys. We are also grateful to the many social services and education departments that invited us to present our findings and used them to inform policy documents and practice guidance.

Our greatest debt is to our research participants, the young people who generously gave their time on many occasions to talk with us and share their experiences of care, school and higher education. We hope that as a result of their help many more young people who have spent time in care will follow in their footsteps and encounter fewer problems.

Sonia Jackson, Sarah Ajayi and Margaret Quigley

Note: All names of young people used in this report are pseudonyms. Some details have been changed to avoid identifying individuals.

Summary

1. PURPOSE AND CONTENT OF THE REPORT

This is the final report of a five-year action research project commissioned by the Frank Buttle Trust to explore the experiences of the small minority of care leavers who continue into higher education. The principal aim of the project was to use this evidence to advise government, local authorities, universities and colleges in order to:

- increase the numbers of young people in care going to university
- enable them to make the most of their time there and to complete their courses successfully
- help local authorities to fulfil their obligations as corporate parents
- raise awareness of the particular needs of this group of students.

During the time when the research was carried out the education of children and young people in public care rose high on the Government's agenda and two major pieces of legislation passed through Parliament, providing a propitious climate for the study and the dissemination of its findings. Under the Children (Leaving Care) Act 2000 (CLCA) local authorities now have a statutory obligation to provide financial support and personal support up to the age of 24 for young people formerly in care who are in full-time education. The Children Act 2004 for the first time lays a duty on local authorities to promote the educational achievement of children they look after.

2. THE RESEARCH PROCESS

Following a preliminary study to establish the feasibility of the research design, the fieldwork stage of the study consisted of recruiting three successive cohorts of 50 care leavers planning to continue into higher education. The first group was followed throughout their three-year degree courses, the second group for two years and the third group for their first year. Participants were interviewed on several occasions and also took part in a number of group events organised by the research team and the Frank Buttle Trust. The majority of the young people remained in contact to the end of the study. The final research sample consisted of 129 young people, by far the largest number of students formerly in care that has ever been studied.

Postal surveys of local authorities and Higher Education Institutions (HEIs) were carried out near the beginning and end of the project. Eleven local authorities acted as an ongoing reference group with representatives interviewed annually. Interim findings were published and shared with central and local government. After completion of the study an extensive dissemination programme was made possible by the award of an additional grant from the KPMG Foundation.

3. PARTICIPANTS IN THE PROJECT

Geographical distribution, gender, ethnicity, family background, reasons for coming into care, age of entry and educational qualifications were compared with the care population generally.

The participants were all volunteers, mainly nominated by local authority lead officers for the education of looked after children or by after care workers. They came from all over England, with the highest proportion of nominations received from London boroughs.

Women outnumbered men in all cohorts, though less so among those coming from overseas. Just under half of the participants were white British but minority ethnic groups were over-represented in the study sample by comparison with the total care population (Figure 3.2).

Figure 3.2: Ethnicity of participants

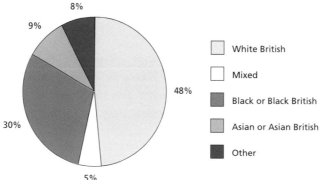

The family backgrounds of UK-born participants and reasons for coming into care were similar to those of other children in care. Sixty per cent of the research sample had suffered abuse or neglect before coming into care, almost exactly the same proportion as in the care population generally. Sixteen per cent of the participants were unaccompanied asylum-seekers. In the third cohort 40 per cent had been born overseas. Compared with UK participants they were rather more likely to have birth parents who were better educated and in higher level occupations.

4. CARE AND EDUCATION BEFORE UNIVERSITY

A full care and educational history was obtained from every participant. Some were critical of aspects of their care experience, especially in residential units, but on balance coming into care was regarded as beneficial. The majority of participants had spent over five years in care and at least one placement had been helpful to their education. Young people who had been placed in a foster family with a strong commitment to supporting education considered this a key factor in their educational success. The quality of the final placement seemed to be more important than the overall number of placements, which ranged from two to 33 (Figure 4.1). Nearly a third of foster carers had studied at degree level and 31 per cent of foster mothers worked in managerial, professional or related occupations.

Figure 4.1: Number of care placements by cohort

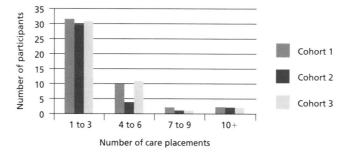

A number of respondents had suffered abuse and discrimination in foster care, but in general foster placements offered a much better educational environment than residential care.

Many young people had missed periods of school before coming into care and this caused problems later. However, once in care, the majority attended school regularly and did well (Figure 4.2). Their GCSE performance was close to the national average, although a high proportion moved to further education colleges rather than continuing at school in Years 12 and 13. Seventy per cent in Cohorts 1 and 2 and 91 per cent in Cohort 3 obtained five or more A*–C passes at GCSE compared with 6 per cent of all looked after children at the time.

Figure 4.2: Educational attainment by cohort

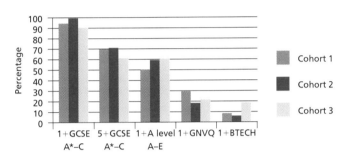

By Degrees participants were highly motivated to do well at school, which differentiated them from many other young people in care. A positive attitude to education might come from their birth family, their foster carer, friends and siblings, or the school itself. Many of the students described themselves as self-motivated and had shown extreme determination to overcome difficulties and achieve their objectives.

The main problems identified by participants at the point of application to university were lack of information and advice when choosing universities and courses; changes of placement during preparation for examinations; uncertainty about available financial support, and anxiety about accommodation during term time and vacations.

5. THE EXPERIENCE OF UNIVERSITY

Students who did not have supportive foster carers often felt very much alone during their early weeks. Some had difficulty processing the information provided and missed the chance to apply for grants for which they were eligible. Making friends at an early stage was extremely important and was easier for those with places in halls of residence. A number of students missed this opportunity due to delays in local authority decisions about funding. In the second and third years most participants moved into shared houses or flats.

Some students, especially in London, stayed in council houses or flats that they were allocated on leaving care. This seriously restricted their choice of course and university. If their accommodation was distant from the institution where they were studying this adversely affected their social relations and inhibited their participation in university life. Council flats were of variable quality and there were failures of communication between Housing and Social Services Departments.

Most participants became more skilled at budgeting during their second and third years but still suffered from a constant shortage of money. Their main source of debt was the student loan and bank overdrafts; credit card debts were much rarer. Almost all took out the maximum student loan every year and after three years their average level of debt was £11,235, compared with the national average of £9,210. One owed up to £20,000. They were usually obliged to take jobs in supermarkets or bars throughout every vacation, including the summer, and few could afford holidays. Students who did not receive enough financial support from their local authority often took on too much paid work and this conflicted with academic demands and might result in failure to submit assignments or inadequate preparation for examinations. Lack of money also limited their social activities and prevented them from engaging fully in university life.

The majority completed their courses successfully or are still continuing their studies. However, difficulties with coursework and dissertations were common, often attributed to earlier gaps in schooling or never having had an established routine of sitting down to do homework after school. More serious problems arose from emotional and relationship issues. Some had to resit examinations or resubmit assignments and several had to carry forward modules into a subsequent year.

Most participants looking back over their university experience said that they had thoroughly enjoyed it and learnt a great deal. They felt it had given them an opportunity to mature and acquire social and life skills. They were vividly aware of the advantages that their education had brought them compared with other young people in care.

6. DROPPING OUT OR HANGING ON

A special study was made of the minority of respondents who decided against taking up their university places or failed to complete their courses. Some participants never got started because they did not achieve the required grades and no one was available to advise them. The drop-out rate for *By Degrees* participants was 10 per cent compared with the national average of 14 per cent.

The main sources of stress were shortage of money, fear of debt, psychological problems arising from care and pre-care experiences, academic difficulties, relationship problems, upsets in birth or foster family, isolation and lack of emotional support. Students were most in danger of dropping out when three or more of these factors coincided. Difficulties in contacting social services caused extreme frustration. Participants with problems did not get appropriate help from Student Support Services in their institution and many had no contact with personal tutors.

The majority showed themselves to be very resilient and persisted with their studies regardless of poverty, ill health and family problems (Figure 5.3). Fewer participants in Cohorts 2 and 3 left prematurely, possibly reflecting better support from local authorities following implementation of the CLCA.

Figure 5.3: Cohort 1: outcomes after three years

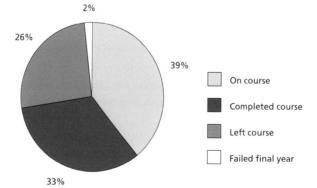

7. COMING FROM OVERSEAS

Young people born in countries outside the UK made up an increasing proportion of the research sample, amounting to 41 per cent in the third cohort. Sixteen per cent were unaccompanied asylum-seekers compared with only 5 per cent in the care population. Some young people travelled with paid agents who quickly deserted them, leaving them vulnerable to exploitation.

Participants from overseas usually had clear educational goals and were highly motivated to aim for university. Most reported that their parents had impressed on them the overriding importance of educational success for their future life chances.

Despite having suffered extreme trauma and adversity none dropped out, except one in his second year of university who was refused permission to stay. They tended to be more focused on their studies and in many cases worked much harder than UK-born students with a care background, putting in on average twice as many hours of private study. Seventy-two per cent of asylum-seeking students were awaiting status decisions and feared repatriation. In some cases they received very inadequate support from their local authorities.

8. THE LOCAL AUTHORITY AS CORPORATE PARENT

The CLCA lays a duty on local authorities to provide financial support and accommodation for young people in full-time education, and to inform them of their entitlement. Unfortunately, the Guidance to the Act (DfES 2003c) includes a clause that in practice allows local authorities to differ widely in the level of support they provide.

An important aim of the project was to assess how far the CLCA had improved the level of support offered by local authorities to care leavers going to university. Comparison of responses from the two surveys carried out three years apart together with the longitudinal study of 12 local authorities showed that progress had been made at the policy level but that there were still wide variations in practice between different authorities and even within the same one.

More local authorities have established procedures and written protocols that can be accessed by young people in care. They are more willing than in 2001 to provide educational equipment, especially computers. The proportion extending foster placements or converting them to supported lodgings has gone up.

Cohort 3 fared considerably better than Cohort 1, who were not covered by the CLCA, and their lower drop-out rate may reflect this improved support.

On the negative side, only a minority of local authorities offered continuing personal and emotional support from a named person or Personal Adviser into the second and third years. In most cases the level of financial support provided fell well short of the benchmark figures used by the Frank Buttle Trust in assessing grant eligibility (see Appendix 5).

The large number of unaccompanied young asylum-seekers aspiring to higher education created resource problems for some authorities in London and the South East.

9. WIDENING PARTICIPATION

Judging from our second survey of HEIs, Government initiatives designed to increase the numbers of disadvantaged young people going to university do not appear to have raised awareness of the needs of care leavers to any appreciable extent. Most HEIs now have officers in post with a widening participation remit. However, very few of those who responded to the questionnaire had any special provision in place for applicants or students with a care background and there seemed to have been little change over three years.

Various kinds of outreach programmes had developed between the first and second *By Degrees* surveys, but only one university is known to have a comprehensive policy relating to care leavers. Ninety-five per cent do not offer any pastoral support to students known to have been in care.

Although participants attended 68 different universities and colleges, there is still a general view that young people in care are not capable of reaching a sufficient educational standard to benefit from higher education.

Some respondents said it would be helpful to know if people applying for places were or had been in care. Seventy-seven per cent of the research participants, with some reservations, said they would have been willing to tick a box on the UCAS form if one had been available.

10. CONCLUSIONS

The *By Degrees* research has provided important new information on a group of young people never previously studied. The findings have implications not only for the small number who at present go on to higher education but for the education and well-being of all children in care.

The research participants felt that they had obtained many benefits from their involvement in the project and were very appreciative of the way the study had been conducted by the research team. They were very keen that the information and experiences that they had shared with the researchers should be used to encourage more young people in care to aim for university. They thought the Government should insist on full implementation of the Children (Leaving Care) Act 2000 so that all young people who had been in care, wherever they came from, would receive adequate support from their local authority. The recommendations in the report are informed by the views expressed by all the young people who took part in the project.

11. MAIN RECOMMENDATIONS

1. Local authorities should plan and budget to support increasing numbers of care leavers going to university.
2. Financial support for care leavers at university should be tailored to their needs and not provided only at a minimum level.
3. Children in care should be enrolled in schools where a high proportion of pupils go to university.
4. There should be a full discussion of post-16 plans before GCSE, including the option of continuing to higher education.
5. Foster carers should be trained and funded to provide accommodation and support for young people during the examination years and throughout their higher education courses.
6. The UCAS form should include an optional tick-box to indicate that an applicant has been in local authority care.
7. Prospective students should be given a written contract specifying the financial and other support to be provided based on discussion of their individual needs and circumstances.
8. Students should be advised and supported to live in university accommodation for the first year.
9. Every student should have a named Personal Adviser for the duration of their course.
10. All HEIs should have a comprehensive policy for recruitment, retention and support of students from a care background.
11. Admissions tutors and widening participation officers should be better informed about the care system.
12. The Government should fund local authorities to support the education of unaccompanied minors seeking asylum. Local authorities should provide skilled support and advice on status problems and ensure high quality legal representation in case of need.

Tables and figures

① Introduction

This report describes the experiences of a group of young people about whom previously nothing was known – the tiny minority of young people in care who succeed in moving into higher education. There are no national figures on how many university students have spent time in care during their childhood nor on what proportion of children looked after by local authorities go to university but the best estimate is about 1 per cent (Social Exclusion Unit 2003). Many local authorities have never had the experience of launching a young person in their care into higher education.

Research on the education of children in care was almost non-existent until the 1990s and although the subject has attracted more interest lately, most of the findings paint an extremely depressing picture. The only research study that focused on ex-care people who had been successful educationally showed that leaving care with even modest educational qualifications made a big difference to the future life chances of the research subjects compared with a matched sample of their peers (Jackson and Martin 1998). Those who continued their studies to tertiary level, however, needed exceptional persistence and powers of endurance. Lacking support from social services, they had to work long hours for low wages in addition to their academic work, often went hungry and found themselves homeless during vacations. One young woman spent the Christmas of her first year at college sleeping in a railway station.

It was stories like these that inspired the Frank Buttle Trust to commission the present study. The Trust has a long history of providing grant aid to children in adversity and those lacking family support, and particularly of promoting their education. One aspect of the Trust's grant aid programme is to support students and trainees in further and higher education, and from this experience grew a strategic aim to gather information which might influence policy and practice more broadly.

THE EDUCATION OF CHILDREN IN CARE

Throughout the last 20 years of the twentieth century, the evidence was becoming increasingly compelling that looked after children were being failed by the education and care systems (Jackson 1987; Fletcher-Campbell and Hall 1990; Borland *et al.* 1998; Jackson and Sachdev 2001; Harker *et al.* 2004). When national figures started to be collected the extent of the failure became apparent for the first time. The clearest indicator was the high proportion of looked after children still leaving care with no qualifications of any kind. The majority still do not even have the opportunity to sit public examinations, and only 8 per cent (an improvement on previous figures) obtained five or more 'good' GCSE passes at grades A*–C in 2003, compared with more than half of all children (DfES 2004).

Statistics of looked after children's performance at key stage national assessments show a steady deterioration relative to other children. Moreover, children in care are at least ten times more likely to be permanently excluded from school and relegated to Pupil Referral Units, receive a few hours a week of home tuition, or be lost to the education system altogether. In response to this evidence, together with earlier reports by the Social Services and Education Inspectorate (SSI and Ofsted 1995), and Sir William Utting's safeguards review, *People Like Us* (1997), the Prime Minister, Tony Blair, asked the Social Exclusion Unit (SEU) to undertake an enquiry into the education of children in care with the objective of finding ways to bring their educational outcomes closer to the performance of children generally.

The report, *A Better Education for Children in Care* (SEU 2003), was published simultaneously with the government Green Paper *Every Child Matters* (DfES 2003a) which together provided the basis for the Children Act 2004. This is a milestone in children's legislation because for the first time it lays a specific duty on local authorities to promote the educational achievement of children they look after.[1]

THE RIGHT TO HIGHER EDUCATION

The Guidance to the Children Act 1989 clearly states that children in care have the same rights to further and higher education as all other children (Department of Health 1991a, b), but in the absence of any duty for local authorities to provide financial support this remained no more than an aspiration until the implementation of the Children (Leaving Care) Act 2000 (CLCA). This Act created a statutory basis for post-care services and for continuing financial support for care leavers beyond the minimum school-leaving age. Those in full-time education are now entitled to support up to the age of 24.

Progress at the legislative and policy level since 1997 has been impressive. The question is how far this is reflected in local authority practice and the experience of young people leaving care. That was what the *By Degrees* study set out to discover.

THE PURPOSE OF THE RESEARCH

The *By Degrees* research project had some distinctive features. First, it was conceived as action research with the intention of helping to shape local and central government policy as it progressed, rather than waiting to make recommendations after the work was completed. Secondly, the funding for the project included a significant portion earmarked for grant aid to the participating students. Thirdly, the study was longitudinal in design, extending to over five years in total. But perhaps the most unusual aspect of the research was the close collaboration between the commissioning body and the researchers. Throughout the study the project team, consisting of the three academic researchers, the Chief Executive, Senior Caseworker and, later, the Head of Development of the Trust met almost monthly to review progress and formulate plans. This had the advantage of ensuring that the objectives of the project were always kept firmly in view and that the research was informed by the depth of experience held by the staff of the Trust.

AIMS OF THE PROJECT

The principal aims of the project were:

- to increase the proportion of young people in care who access higher education
- to enable them to make the most of their time at university and to complete their courses successfully
- to help local authorities fulfil their obligations as corporate parents by providing information on the financial, practical and emotional support that care leavers may need to achieve similar educational outcomes to young people in the general population
- to make more widely known the extraordinary experiences that many care leavers face on their journey to higher education
- to raise awareness among higher education institutions (HEIs) of the particular needs of this group of students.

One important aspect of the study was to explore local authority policy and practice in relation to care leavers aiming for or attending university. The project was set up just when the CLCA was completing its passage through Parliament so that a further objective was to assess how far the Act had influenced thinking and changed provision for this group of young people.

A second part of the study shifted the focus to universities and colleges. During the progress of the research, the issue of widening participation to make higher education more accessible to young people from disadvantaged backgrounds rose very high on the political agenda. But to what extent did this include care leavers? And what special provision, if any, was made for students with no families to fall back on in times of trouble?

EXPLORING THE STUDENT EXPERIENCE

However, the main purpose of the research was to explore the experience of the young people themselves from their own perspective. Our research participants had reached an educational level well within normal expectations for half the school population but highly unusual for children in public care. How far did their local authority recognise and celebrate this achievement? If we could identify the factors that contributed to the success of this small group of care leavers it would have important implications for the education of children in care more generally.

Once the ex-care students arrived at university how were they able to support themselves? We wanted to find out what were the main difficulties they faced and how they coped with them. Did they continue to be successful academically? Did they enjoy themselves? Anecdotal evidence suggested that there might be a high drop-out rate. It was important to discover how many were able to complete their courses and, if not, what had caused them to leave prematurely.

All these questions were addressed in the course of the research, and although we cannot claim to have discovered all the answers we believe that our findings have an important contribution to make towards improving the life chances of all children in care, not only the few who at present go on to higher education.

KEY FACTS

- One care leaver in a hundred goes to university compared with 43 per cent of all children.
- The *By Degrees* study was commissioned by the Frank Buttle Trust to find out ways in which this proportion could be increased.
- The study was designed to explore the experience of care leavers at university, local authority policy and practice and the plans of higher education institutions (HEIs) in relation to widening participation and supporting students with a care background.
- The Children Act 2004 for the first time lays a duty on local authorities to promote the education of children they look after.

NOTE

1. The relevant clause in the Children Act 2004 Chapter 31 Part 5 (52) reads:

    The duty of a local authority under subsection (3)(a) [Section 22 of the Children Act 1989] to safeguard and promote the welfare of a child looked after by them includes in particular a duty to promote the child's educational achievement.

2 *The research process*

The limited previous research into the lives of young people with a care background accessing university places had identified a number of persistent problems. These included: a lack of information and guidance for care leavers aiming to continue in education after leaving care; low expectations and little encouragement from social workers; unwillingness by social services to provide a realistic level of financial assistance; difficulty in finding accommodation, particularly during vacations; problems in meeting educational expenses; and the absence of any system of continuing personal support (Jackson and Martin, 1998; Martin and Jackson, 2002). There was no certainty that such experiences were typical, however, since these were small-scale retrospective studies and some of the participants had been in care at a time when services and expectations were very different.

THE FEASIBILITY STUDY

Because so little was known about young people going to university from care, the first stage of the research was to find out if it would be possible to recruit a reasonable number of research subjects. The feasibility study was carried out by Sonia Jackson and Susan Roberts at the University of Wales Swansea and consisted of a survey of local authorities in England and Wales and telephone interviews with a small number of university students who had been in care (Jackson and Roberts, 2000).

They contacted 215 Directors of Social Services with a request for information on the numbers of care leavers in their authority currently on degree-level courses. Of the 68 who replied, most explained that the figures could only be estimates since, unless the young person was receiving financial assistance from the local authority, communication was usually lost. By extrapolating from the figures received, it was calculated that the projected sample of 50 young people in three successive cohorts would not be an unreasonable aim.

The interviews provided ample evidence of the need for the *By Degrees* project. They confirmed our impressions from earlier research and the experience of the Frank Buttle Trust that young people moving into higher education from care face severe problems. These included:

- low expectations and little encouragement from social workers
- a shortage of information and guidance for care leavers aiming to continue in education after leaving care
- lack of financial support from local authorities
- difficulty in maintaining accommodation during term time and vacations
- problems in meeting normal educational expenses such as books, stationery, computer supplies and technical equipment required for the course.

On the basis of the pilot study a formal proposal was submitted to the Trustees of the Frank Buttle Trust, who agreed to seek to raise the necessary funds and commission the research. It was decided that it would be appropriate to base the study at the Institute of Education, University of London, where Sonia Jackson was already a Visiting Professorial

Fellow. An Advisory Group, chaired by Sir William Utting, was set up and met regularly throughout the fieldwork phase of the project (see Appendix 2).

DESIGN OF THE STUDY

For the purposes of the research, three successive cohorts of participants were recruited, mainly through local authorities, although some volunteered independently or were referred by the Frank Buttle Trust caseworker. The first cohort was tracked throughout their university career, the second group for two years and the third for their first year only. Because the participants were self-selected it was not possible to recruit a representative sample, but having three groups for purposes of comparison reduced the risk of drawing misleading conclusions from one atypical year group. Following the first group for nearly four years gave the researchers a unique opportunity to understand how previous and current experiences contributed to the process and outcomes of their university careers.

THE LOCAL AUTHORITY SURVEYS

As already mentioned, the CLCA completed its passage through Parliament just before the start of the main study in January 2001. It was not implemented until the following year, providing an opportunity to compare the services received by the first cohort to whom the Act did not apply, with what local authorities provided for the second and third cohorts who started their courses after the Act came into force.

In order to do this, a postal questionnaire was sent to all local authorities in England and Wales in the first year of the project and again in the fourth year. In addition, 12 authorities agreed to act as an ongoing reference group. We used the percentages of young people leaving care with five or more GCSE passes at grades A*–C as our selection criterion, and chose four authorities with low percentages, four with comparatively high percentages and four where attainment was average. Representatives from this core group of authorities were interviewed at yearly intervals, although one authority dropped out at an early stage. The findings from this part of the study are reported in Chapter 8.

HIGHER EDUCATION INSTITUTIONS (HEIs)

One further strand of the project was a survey of all universities, Oxford and Cambridge colleges, and other HEIs. This aimed to find out how many were aware of applicants and students with a care background as a discrete group who might need special consideration, and to identify any initiatives designed to support them. Significantly, the survey was conducted in the context of the Government's agenda of widening access to universities for young people from areas with a low proportion of university entrants or from families with no tradition or experience of higher education (see Chapter 9).

RECRUITING PARTICIPANTS

All the research participants in the study were volunteers and were recruited initially through local authority leaving care and after-care teams, or by contacting lead officers for the education of looked after children. The criteria for inclusion were that they had been in local authority care at the age of 16 and that they had been offered a place on a degree-level course.

Based on estimates from the earlier feasibility study, the project aimed to identify 50 participants among students entering higher education in each of the academic years 2001–2, 2002–3 and 2003–4. Although an ambitious target, with the cooperation of the leaving care and post-16 teams, it was possible to recruit above this number in each year, though not all completed their courses or even made it to the starting post. Some of those nominated turned out not to meet the criteria for inclusion, either because they had not been in care at 16 or they were not studying on degree-level courses. In some cases we were unsuccessful in contacting the nominees using the addresses and telephone numbers given by their local authorities and never managed to locate them. Indeed, sustaining contact with the participants involved a major expenditure of time and effort throughout the project.

Despite many difficulties, however, we were able to remain in touch with the majority of the students included in the study. The final research sample of 129 (all three cohorts) is by far the largest group of educationally successful young people in care that has ever been studied. In addition, being able to follow the first group through a full three years provided a unique insight into the way the impact of care, and of the experiences that led up to it, continue to resonate during young adulthood.

RESEARCH METHOD

A similar approach was adopted with all three cohorts. Each volunteer was initially sent a brief questionnaire to collect basic information: ethnicity, educational qualifications, intended course and institution, age first looked after, reasons for entering care, brief details of placements and whether they had any dependents. Subsequently, several contacts by telephone and letter were made before researchers met participants for the first time.

The first interview was unstructured: researchers asked the young person to tell the story of his or her life. An interview guide was used only to ensure that all relevant areas were covered, and the interviewer attempted to follow the unfolding narrative rather than to ask a series of questions. Some interviewees needed more prompting than others, but in general they were eager to talk about themselves and their experiences. Some of the interviews lasted as long as three hours. Many of the young people remarked that they had never before had the chance to tell their story without interruption, despite numerous encounters with social workers. A few participants disclosed for the first time experiences of abuse while they had been in care, perhaps feeling enough distance but also sufficient trust in the researchers to speak openly about painful experiences. And, as one participant told us, 'When you talk about yourself for an hour and a half it's really interesting and it reminds you of things that have been buried, so it's cathartic.'

In most cases the information relevant to the research study emerged spontaneously. This included: what lay behind their exceptional achievement in accessing higher education; their experiences in care and at school; the reasons for the separation from their families; the extent to which being in care had been a help or an obstacle to their educational progress; their most important sources of support; how much they knew about the CLCA and its implications; details of financial and personal support provided by their local authorities and how well they felt this met their needs.

Interviews were tape-recorded, transcribed as far as resources allowed, and analysed using SPSS and the NVivo qualitative data analysis package. Each participant was allocated an assumed name which was used for all recording purposes and publications, with the information kept under secure conditions.

Most of the participants were interviewed twice more using a semi-structured question-naire, once at the end of their first academic year and again during their second year of study. Those who began their degree courses in 2001 were also interviewed after they had graduated. All participants were asked to fill in self-completion questionnaires. In addition to face-to-face interviews, much useful information was obtained from informal telephone conversations throughout the progress of the research and through two focus group discussions.

The project culminated for the participants with a reception hosted by Lord Laming of Tewin at the House of Lords, and sponsored by the KPMG Foundation. This provided an opportunity to celebrate their achievement and for the young people to meet each other and exchange experiences of both care and student life. This event was greatly enjoyed by all those who attended and was often singled out in the final interviews as a highlight of their involvement in the project.

MAKING RESEARCH COUNT

In keeping with the objective of influencing local and national policy and practice, the project team took every opportunity to share emerging findings with policy-makers and relevant professional groups. Two reports were produced at the request of the Social Exclusion Unit and cited in the subsequent report to the Prime Minister (SEU 2003). A substantial interim report on the first cohort was published and launched at a national conference, in which research participants played a prominent role as workshop leaders. They spoke movingly about their own experiences and had a clear perception of what changes were needed. Evaluation of the conference was overwhelmingly favourable, with the contribution of the young people picked out for special appreciation.

The interim report, *By Degrees – The First Year* (Jackson *et al.* 2003), follows the first cohort of 46 university entrants from the time they were offered a place to the end of the following summer vacation. It also reports results from the first survey of local authorities and from the questionnaire to HEIs. The findings are not reviewed here as they are discussed in later chapters in relation to all three cohorts.

The publication of the report aroused great interest and resulted in many invitations to speak in all parts of the UK (see Appendix 4). The recommendations from the interim report are summarised in Appendix 1.

KEY FACTS

- Following a feasibility study, three successive cohorts of students who had been in care at the age of 16 were recruited and tracked through their university courses.
- The final research sample consisted of 129 young people, by far the largest number of students formerly in care that has ever been studied.
- Parallel studies of local authorities and HEIs were carried out.
- Interim findings were published and shared with central and local government.

3 The participants

Since it was not possible to select the research group to form a representative sample of looked after children, it was important to find out if the participants in the project were unusual in some way. We looked at geographical distribution, gender, ethnicity, family background, reasons for coming into care, age of entry, and educational qualifications. Where possible we compared the characteristics of the students in the three cohorts with those of the care population generally.

The largest single group of students in all cohorts came from London boroughs but there was a good spread of participants from all over England, as shown in Figure 3.1. Outside London a majority of students in the first cohort were drawn from northern authorities, whereas in the second cohort they came predominantly from southern authorities. In the third cohort this imbalance was even more marked, due to the high proportion of volunteers coming from outside the UK who were more likely to be placed in southern counties. Although students from Wales were eligible to take part we did not have any representatives from Welsh unitary authorities.

In all cohorts women outnumbered men and this was true across all ethnic categories. There were twice as many women as men in the first cohort and three times as many in the second. The third cohort was 70 per cent female. There are probably a number of reasons for this. Studies relying on volunteers almost invariably find women over-represented (Jackson and Martin 1998). Girls do better than boys educationally, both in the care and non-care populations (DfES 2003b). A third factor is that girls have a higher chance of being fostered than boys, and foster care is far more likely to offer an environment conducive to educational success, as we show later. Among those who came to the UK as asylum-seekers the gender balance was more equal.

Figure 3.1: Regions where participants came from

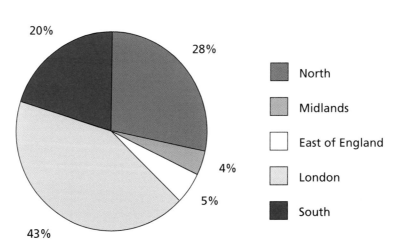

ETHNICITY

The most striking difference between our research group and the care population generally was the higher proportion from minority ethnic backgrounds, which was even more marked in the second and third cohorts. Figure 3.2 shows the ethnicity of research participants in all three cohorts.

As in the care population generally, the highest proportion of participants (47 per cent averaged over the three cohorts) fell into the category White British. Yet, although the number of children entering the care system from minority ethnic and mixed ethnicity families is growing, they were still over-represented in the study sample. The majority of Black students in the study were of African rather than Caribbean origin. Importantly, a significant number of participants had come to Britain as refugees or asylum-seekers and 16 per cent of the whole cohort had been unaccompanied. Most of them were African but there were also a number of young people from other European countries. The characteristics and experience of this group often differed markedly from those of young people who were born and brought up in the UK (see Chapter 7).

FAMILY BACKGROUND

It was often difficult to obtain precise information about the birth families of participants. Either they were very young when they came into care and social workers had not been assiduous in constructing life story books, or the interviewees preferred not to dwell on unhappy experiences. Young people were asked about the occupations and educational qualifications of their fathers and mothers at the time when the respondent first left their family. There were some differences between young people from overseas and those born within the UK. Overseas students were rather more likely to have parents with experience of higher education; almost a third of their mothers and 45 per cent of fathers had higher educational qualifications compared with only 25 per cent of fathers and 26 per cent of mothers of home students. These findings are discussed further in Chapter 7.

The general picture presented by the participants' accounts of their birth families was one of extreme volatility, with many house moves, changes of partners, new people joining or leaving the household, constant turmoil and upheaval. Many participants described difficult relationships with step-parents. Domestic violence and physical or sexual abuse were a feature of many accounts. One young woman had spent six months in hospital as a four-year-old after being dropped into a hot bath by her mother as a punishment. Emotional abuse and scapegoating were also common. Other parents were said to be well-meaning but unable to function effectively due to mental illness or drug and/or alcohol problems. Many

Figure 3.2: Ethnicity of participants[1]

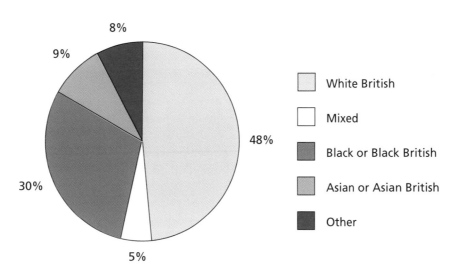

of the young people displayed remarkable understanding and compassion for their parents and continued to feel affection for them. A young man whose mother's alcohol addiction eventually led to her death told us:

> *We always knew she loved us and she cared very much about our education whenever she wasn't drinking.*

Sometimes a parent seemed to have entered a calmer phase of life after the period of turbulence which led to their child coming into care.

> *I couldn't get on with my mum when I was younger, but now she's my best friend.*

It certainly could not be said that these young people had enjoyed an easier childhood than other children in care. Their family background was very similar to what is known of the care population generally (Bebbington and Miles 1989). Among the participants were many who had family or personal experience of murder, suicide, psychotic illness, drug overdose, arson and even genocide, and a very high proportion who had suffered abuse or severe neglect.

A few of the young people had made a deliberate decision to have nothing more to do with either of their birth parents and had not seen them for many years, but they were in a minority. Most of the UK students had contact with one or more birth relatives (not necessarily parents) and were on reasonably good terms with them, though they were usually quite clear that they did not want to live with them. Birth relatives were named as an important source of personal and emotional support by 27 per cent of the sample.

Maureen was the only child of a heroin addict and came into care aged nine when her mother died of AIDS. Maureen experienced extreme privation as a young child. She remembered one Christmas when all they had to eat were the chocolate decorations off the tree. However, she also remembered that her great treat when she lived with her mother was a trip to a bookshop, and during the six months when she did not go to school 'my entire life was inside books'.

COMING INTO CARE It was not always easy to find out what had led to the need for the young people to leave their birth families Those who had come into care when they were young often knew very little about their early lives. They also had mixed reactions to discussing what had usually been a distressing period. Some preferred to put unpleasant experiences as far behind them as possible, others related the facts as they knew them without apparent emotion, while still others broke down in tears and occasionally felt they could not go on with the interview.

Hannah was sexually abused by her brother from the age of 11 and took repeated overdoses to draw attention to her plight. However, several times she was returned to her mother who was physically violent towards her, refusing to believe her story. Finally she went up to two women police officers in the street and begged them to take her to social services who found the first of what was to be a series of foster homes.

The reasons for coming into care for all cohorts corresponded closely with those given for the care population in official statistics and are presented for Cohorts 2 and 3 in Figure 3.3.

Figure 3.3: Main reasons for coming into care (Cohorts 2 and 3)

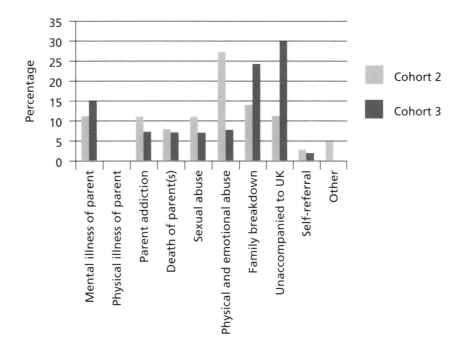

For those who first came into care in their teenage years, self-referral was quite common, and some young people reported making several attempts to escape from abusive families before they were accepted for care by social services. Seventy-eight per cent of participants in Cohort 1 had suffered abuse even if it was not the main reason for care. For about a quarter of participants in the second and third cohorts this was the main cause of coming into care. Excluding asylum-seekers, nearly two-thirds had been abused by parents or step-parents. Over the whole *By Degrees* sample, 60 per cent reported having experienced some form of abuse or neglect; national figures show that this is true of 62 per cent of those in the care population.

> Samantha's mother suffered from paranoid schizophrenia and her father from a diagnosed personality disorder. They repeatedly separated and came together again and Samantha was often caught up in violent conflicts between them. The family was well known to social services but Samantha was only taken into care, aged 14, when she confided in a schoolteacher that her home life was unbearable. 'I was very low emotionally – the fighting took it out of me.' She was fortunate to be placed in a foster home which she described as 'a stable, happy environment' and where she formed a strong attachment to her foster family.

A high proportion of birth parents of young people in our sample had severe mental disorders, and the pattern of repeated short-term admissions to care was a common one. It seemed that the commendable objective of returning children to their families was sometimes pursued regardless of the child's wishes or the medical prognosis.

KEY FACTS

- Participants came from all over England, but more were from London boroughs.
- Women outnumbered men in all cohorts.
- Minority ethnic groups were over-represented by comparison with the overall care population.
- Sixteen per cent were unaccompanied asylum-seekers; 40 per cent of the third cohort were born overseas.
- Family background was very similar to all children in care.
- Sixty per cent had suffered abuse or neglect.
- Twenty-seven per cent named birth relatives as an important source of support.

NOTE

1. In some cases, young people described their own ethnicity in a way that did not correspond with the information they gave during their interview. This may have been due to a wish to distance themselves from an absent or abusive parent, or to a sense of not belonging to a particular culture or ethnic group. We accepted their own attribution and the numbers were too small to affect the overall picture.

4 Care and education before *university*

In order to find out whether *By Degrees* participants had experiences of care that were very different from those of other looked after children we asked them to describe their time in care in as much detail as possible. For each young person a full care history was obtained and more specific questions were asked about the first and last placements, or the most important placement from the respondent's viewpoint.

STABILITY The majority of participants had spent over five years in care, so their care experience could be considered to have made a positive contribution to their educational success. Almost all acknowledged this explicitly, reporting that they would never have got to university if they had remained with their birth families. The exceptions were those who had come from overseas, who usually said that their parents had impressed on them the importance of education and had given them support and encouragement up to the time of their separation. However, although their motivation might have come from their families, the practical means to continue their education depended on the local authority in which they found themselves.

The research evidence with regard to how much placement stability contributes to educational attainment is somewhat unclear (Jackson and Thomas 2001). Reducing placement movement was one of the key aims of the Government's *Quality Protects* programme (Department of Health 1998), but many authorities failed to meet the modest target of no more than 16 per cent of children having three or more placement changes in one year. Figure 4.1 shows the number of placements for participants in all three cohorts. Relative to other young people in care, therefore, our participants did seem to have enjoyed rather more stable care careers, with just over half having one or two placements, of which at least one lasted several years. Since the peak ages for entry into care for the research group were 14

Figure 4.1: Number of care placements by cohort

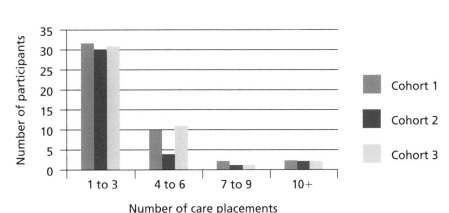

and 15 years, and placement breakdowns most frequently occur during adolescence, this degree of stability was unusual (Triseliotis *et al.* 1995).

From the participants' own accounts there was no doubt that a stable long-term foster home was a great advantage, both educationally and emotionally, even when they came to it relatively late and after a series of less successful placements. For example Boris and his elder brother had a particularly traumatic family history and went through seven different foster homes before they were eventually placed with a single woman with a grown-up family, where they settled happily and from which they both went on to university.

For some young people who were moved many times school was the one fixed point and a refuge from the problems of home and care. Having multiple placements did not necessarily rule out educational success.

Jade was rejected by her mother and put into care at the age of four. In total she had 33 placements. Sometimes she went back to the same foster placement or a relative and sometimes to her grandmother. She had two unhappy residential placements and was physically and sexually abused in a children's home which was closed down as a result. During this time she went through a period of self-harming. She missed a whole year of school and altogether attended five different ones, in some of which she was bullied and suffered discrimination. Despite this she always liked school because 'it was the most stable thing I had'. Although she felt that she would have done much better had she stayed in one place and at one school, she still managed to obtain six GCSE passes at grades A*–C (one being A*) and three grades D–G. She obtained four B grades at A/S level and two C's and a B at A-level.

When everything else fell apart I focused on school.

Her determination to succeed came partly from her aspiration to be a solicitor from the age of 11 years, but most of all because she didn't want to end up like her mother.

RESIDENTIAL CARE   Almost a third of the participants spent time in residential units during their care career, but for most it was a transient experience. Only one person in the first cohort went directly from a children's home to university. This is further testimony to previous research demonstrating that the majority of children's homes offer a poor educational environment and little encouragement to succeed at school (Brown *et al.* 1998; Berridge and Brodie 1998; Utting 1997; Brodie 2003; Gallagher *et al.* 2004). Many of our respondents commented that during their time in residential care they differed from the other young people living there in wanting to do well in their schoolwork.

Steven spoke warmly of the head of the home where he spent three years but had nothing good to say of it otherwise:

> *I was the only child in the home who went to school. I had work to do and the other kids would be kicking off, sometimes all night, and I had to go to school in the mornings. The others had no motivation. The staff didn't push them. . . . The only person who helped me was the only educated one, the one with a degree.*

Fiona's view was similar:

> *My problem was just, like, I was doing A-levels, everyone else was on the dole. They played their music full blast and didn't care about me studying. And then we had to share the kitchen and cleaning duties and I was the only one who did my bit. . . .*

One young woman, who played a very active role in groups for looked after children in her local area, attributed her own success to having placements only in foster care:

> *I've been lucky in that I haven't been in children's homes. I think that's the most important thing.*

In her opinion placement in residential care was equivalent to 'being thrown on the educational scrapheap'.

However, in another case a good residential placement rescued a young woman who had been severely abused and was going through a very wild phase in her life. She became strongly attached to the staff of the children's home where she was placed, although she later moved to a foster family where she continued to live while attending college and university. Now in her third year studying leisure and tourism, she still visits the residential home regularly and named one of the care staff there as an important source of support.

FOSTER CARE   Foster care presented a very much more mixed picture. In many cases foster carers were said to have provided consistent support and encouragement for education. Perhaps most importantly they often had high expectations for the young people they looked after. They insisted on regular school attendance, advocated for the young person if trouble arose, provided congenial study conditions, supervised and helped with homework and often contributed to purchase or upgrading of computers and other equipment. Several interviewees expressed appreciation of the discipline and structure provided by their foster home. On the other hand some made a point of saying that they did not feel pressured and that their foster carers always made it clear that they were free to make their own decisions, offering advice when asked.

Foster carers who had higher educational qualifications themselves almost invariably gave education top priority. However, there seemed to be little difference in attitudes or behaviour between these carers, who were in a minority, and those who, as far as the participant knew, had left school with minimal qualifications. It is noteworthy, however, that in both the second and third cohorts between a quarter and a third of foster carers had studied at degree level. Thirty-one per cent of foster mothers working outside the home were in managerial, professional or associated groups. This contrasts with what we know about foster mothers generally, very few of whom have any educational qualifications and if they are in employment tend to be in unskilled jobs (Triseliotis *et al.* 2000; Pithouse, Lowe and Hill-Tout 2004).

Some of the participants had many problems at school and were seriously behind their age group in academic attainment until they went to live in the foster home which they identified as their most important placement. They had often missed a great deal of school in their early years as a result of the chaotic life-style and frequent moves of their birth families. It was moving to foster care that seemed to have launched them on an upward trajectory, of which regular school attendance was an essential component. Apart from those who came to the UK as refugees, very few of our respondents had been out of school for more than a few days.

In cases where relationships were good, the commitment of the foster carers and the strong emotional bond that formed between them and the young people was probably more important than anything else. Foster carers were almost always named among the five key people in the young person's life. Many participants commented on the closeness of the relationship: 'I class them as my real family'; 'They are my real parents'; 'I call them Mum and Dad'; 'My foster mother is a true friend – I can always talk to her'.

Foster siblings were very often referred to as brothers and sisters, sometimes causing confusion to the interviewers. It is noteworthy that, although the current approved term is 'foster *carer*' most of our respondents made a point of calling their carers 'foster parents', or foster Mum or Dad. As one young man said, 'it sounds more homely'. He seemed also to be making the point that the relationship was one of mutual affection, not simply a practical arrangement. Several participants emphasised that any payment was to compensate foster families on low incomes for the use of a room and the cost of food, not a reward for caring.

Foster carers of this kind gave the young person stability, care and affection and made them feel part of a family. However, we cannot ignore the fact that a number of our participants had negative experiences in foster care. There were instances of physical or sexual abuse in foster placements and some young people were treated quite differently from the foster carer's birth children. One young woman was given different food from the rest of the family and made to eat in a separate room.

It would be quite wrong, therefore, to suggest that foster care was without its problems, but it was usually a final, successful foster placement that enabled the young person to go to university, even if they had had several previous ones where they were not happy.

EDUCATIONAL ATTAINMENT

Although coming into care was generally seen as helpful to their education, young people still faced many obstacles before achieving success. For some, the weakness of their early educational experience created longer-term problems in reaching their academic potential. In a few cases, young people described carers who were not supportive of their wish to go to university, suggesting that they should get a job or take a vocational course instead. At times, they were made to feel by social workers and carers that they were putting too much pressure on themselves, perhaps a reflection of the low expectations of children in care. In some placements, carers reportedly showed more interest in their birth children's education than in that of the foster child. One participant twice requested a change of foster placement because he felt so discouraged by his foster carers' indifference to his school experience.

Unsurprisingly, the *By Degrees* participants had done much better in the later stages of their school career than the majority of the care population. On average the young women in Cohort 1 obtained nine GCSE passes compared with eight for the young men, and the differential increased with the number of subjects taken. Overall, their performance (Figure 4.2) was close to the national picture, although they achieved fewer passes in the A*–C range. However, some of the participants' attainment was outstanding by any criteria. One young woman in Cohort 3 obtained ten GCSE passes, four of them with A* grades, the others all As, and went on to get two As and a B at A level and a place at Oxford University.

> Lee's early life was blighted by domestic violence. When his father committed suicide, his mother became severely depressed. Lee first came into care at the age of 11 and moved backwards and forwards between home and five different foster placements. Eventually he applied to be made subject to a care order to ensure that he would not be returned home again. None of his foster carers was supportive of his education; it was the parents of his best friend at school to whom he turned for encouragement. His GCSE grades were four As and six A*s. He went on to pass four A levels with A grades and is currently studying banking and international finance.

All of the students had continued in education after 16 but over 40 per cent had moved into further education colleges rather than staying at school to take A levels. They were also more likely to have taken vocational GNVQ or BTEC courses. This is significant given that although they are supposed to be equivalent, a much lower proportion of young people with vocational qualifications than those with A levels, go on to university (Newby 2004). Social workers and carers need to be aware of this in order to give young people informed advice at the point when they are deciding what to do after Year 11.

Figure 4.2: Educational attainment by cohort

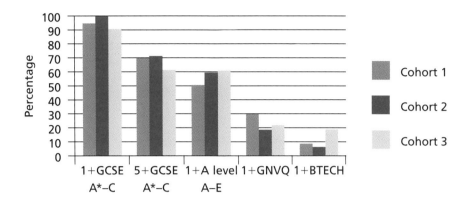

AIMING FOR UNIVERSITY

In discussion with the participants it became clear that their personal motivation and a sense of their own potential were key factors, even when their school performance was depressed by their early experiences and family situation. Some of them told us that they had formed the ambition to go to university at a very early age, as young as seven in one case and four in another.

Those who attended schools where a high proportion of pupils stayed to 18 and moved on to higher education obviously had a significant advantage. For them going to university just seemed the natural thing to do. Their friends were all going and they assumed they would do the same. They described themselves as swept along the academic path to higher education without having to make a conscious decision.

A second group was responsive to the views or experiences of others. They were encouraged by family members and other people they respected, or they followed in the path of older brothers and sisters. Being in a family where foster carers' birth children already had experience of university also encouraged some participants to see it as a normal progression. In particular, as we have already noted, refugees and asylum-seekers tended to come from backgrounds where education was highly valued.

A third group was strongly self-motivated. They wanted to make other people proud of them or to prove that schoolteachers or others who doubted their ability were wrong. Most of all, they had a clear perception that going to university would unlock career and life-style opportunities that would not otherwise be available to them. They often saw this as a means of escape from their family background and the route to a better way of living than their parents.

Motivation proved not only important in getting to university but in staying there and succeeding. Those who planned to go on to higher education for well thought-out reasons were more likely to stay the course. Those who wanted to please others or were simply following in someone else's footsteps were at higher risk of giving up when they encountered difficulties.

For those young people who were successful not only in accessing but staying in higher education, foster families were usually the most important source of motivation and continuing support. Foster mothers were mentioned more frequently, but foster fathers also played an important role, particularly in helping with homework and providing transport. In two cases single women provided supported lodgings for young people over 16 when a previous foster placement broke down. For both, their 'landladies' became friends and provided educational support and encouragement at a crucial time.

Stephanie was asked to leave the foster home where she had lived for seven years when the fostering allowance was ended on her eighteenth birthday, a few weeks before her A level exams. Social services found her lodgings and her landlady, who happened to be a careers adviser, was able to persuade her chosen university to accept her when her results fell short of predictions due to her distress at her abrupt rejection by her former foster carers. Stephanie went on to complete a three-year degree course and qualify as a social worker.

THE IMPORTANCE OF GOOD SCHOOLS

The school is a highly significant influence that is often overlooked in the case of children in care. In the final interview we asked if the young person knew how their secondary school was chosen, and the name of the last one attended and also how they thought it would be rated in the area. A few participants remembered discussions about this, in which birth parents sometimes took a part, but most thought they were just sent to the most convenient or nearest school. Because children often change placement in the middle of a school year they are usually allocated to a school that has unfilled places, which is unlikely to be among the most popular.

We checked the position of the last school attended in the league tables for 2001 and divided the schools into three groups: those where more than 90 per cent of pupils achieved five or more A*–C passes at GCSE, those where more than 50 per cent reached this level and those where fewer than 50 per cent did so. Only four participants attended top-rated schools. Over half of Cohort 2 participants went to schools in the lowest group and nearly half in Cohort 3. This makes their achievement all the more remarkable, but it suggests that social workers should be making far more effort than in the past to obtain places for looked after children in schools where high academic attainment is the norm.

APPLYING FOR COURSES

Young people living independently or in families with no experience of higher education depended heavily on the careers service, web sites, leaflets and brochures for prospective students for their information. University Open Days also played an important role, and some of the participants commented that it was either during or after an open day that they made the decision to go to university. Making their application was not easy without adequate advice from knowledgeable adults. They often had to be very determined to obtain the information they needed about universities and courses and were in danger of choosing subjects or institutions that were unsuited to their interests and abilities, again putting them at risk of dropping out later (see Chapter 6). Looking back, many of the participants commented that they would have gone to a different university or picked a different course if they had been better informed.

Filling in the all-important UCAS (Universities and Colleges Admissions Service) form was another hurdle. The personal statement would have provided an opportunity for the applicant to inform the admissions staff that he or she had been in care, but few of them did so. This was partly because they were uncertain if it would help them or work against them, but also because they were often anxious to leave their care status behind and afraid that the stigma they had experienced in the past might follow them into their new life. However, when asked if they would have been prepared to tick a box on the form if it had been available, 77 per cent answered 'yes'. Some stated firmly that they were not ashamed of having been in care, but a few specified that they would need to be assured that the information would be confidential and would lead to extra support being available.

A further difficulty was filling in forms to apply for financial help from the local authority and answering all the questions about parental occupation and income. There seemed to be no space, one young man explained, for saying that your parents were dead.

However, in practice, all UK students seemed to have had little difficulty in getting their fees paid by their local education authority (LEA).

PROBLEMS   Care leavers faced two major problems that students living at home do not have to worry about: uncertainty about accommodation and not knowing if they would have financial support to enable them to continue their studies.

Some local authorities still pursue a policy of moving young people out of foster care into semi-independent living at 16, which can mean a council flat, a supervised shared house, or in some cases bed and breakfast accommodation. Others automatically terminate foster placements on the young person's eighteenth birthday. One young woman was told that she must find her own accommodation in the middle of her A-level course at a further education college when she was just 17. For others, moves arranged by social services just before examinations were sadly common. Foster carers often wanted to continue providing a home for the young person to stay with them but could not afford the loss of income when the fostering allowance was abruptly withdrawn. Some, however, protested strongly and succeeded in opposing inappropriate moves suggested by social services.

There were striking differences in practice between different local authorities. Some simply continued long-term foster placements for students, including paying foster carers for vacation accommodation, throughout their time at university. More commonly, they ended payments to carers at the point when the student started their university course and paid a rental or living allowance directly to the young person.

Another major problem, especially for students in Cohort 1, was that most local authorities had no agreed policies relating to care leavers in higher education and simply made decisions on an *ad hoc* basis. This often meant referring matters up the hierarchy and waiting for authorisation, which could be slow in coming. Some young people could get no information about what financial support would be forthcoming until a few days before they were due to start their course. In some cases this resulted in their missing the chance of getting a place in a hall of residence and being forced to settle for more expensive and less satisfactory private accommodation.

The turnover of social services staff often resulted in promises being made which were then repudiated when the social worker who made them moved on. Not many young people were as assertive as one respondent who insisted on having precise information in writing on what financial support her local authority was prepared to offer.

Bharti expected to complete her two-year art and design course successfully and was keen to move to another institution where she could continue into a third year for a degree. But at the last interview she was heavily in debt and in fear of eviction, mainly as a result of her local authority persistently failing to make rent payments as had been promised. She was beginning to lose hope and thought she would probably give up and get a job.

There was some evidence that this was less of a problem for the 2003 entrants. By that time many local authority leaving care teams had devolved budgets and were able to use them to support care leavers in higher education under the CLCA. However, some local authorities seemed not to have taken on board their responsibility to provide continuing support up to the age of 24 for those in full-time education.

Financial arrangements are discussed in more detail in Chapters 5 and 8.

KEY
FINDINGS

- The majority of participants had spent over five years in care and at least one placement had been helpful to their education.
- Most *By Degrees* participants had relatively stable care careers but one young woman had 33 placements and said school had provided the only stability in her life.
- Although some respondents had suffered abuse and discrimination in foster care, in general foster placements offered a much better educational environment than residential care.
- Nearly a third of foster carers had studied at degree level and 31 per cent of foster mothers worked in managerial, professional or similar occupations.
- Moving to foster care was associated with regular school attendance and an upward educational trajectory.
- Seventy per cent in Cohorts 1 and 2 and 91 per cent in Cohort 3 obtained five or more A*–C passes in GCSE compared with 6 per cent of all looked after children at the time.
- Forty per cent moved to further education colleges after 16.
- Only four participants attended schools at the top end of the league table.
- Cohort 3 participants had fewer problems in obtaining information and guarantees of support from their local authorities.

5 *The experience of university*

At the time of writing most participants in the first cohort who remained on their courses had completed their degrees or were continuing for a fourth year, those in Cohort 2 had started on their third year and Cohort 3 on their second. The young people who entered university in the autumn of 2001 and made up our first cohort had already embarked on the next stage of their lives and were able to take a more objective overview of the whole experience.

EARLY DAYS Most new students feel some trepidation when arriving at university for the first time, but for *By Degrees* participants these feelings were much more intense. Many of them came from birth and foster families in which no one had previously had experience of higher education and they had no idea what to expect. Three years later Monica still remembered the misery of finding herself in a bare, white-walled room, knowing no one and lost on a large campus with no direction signs. Throughout her first term she felt as if she was 'living in a bubble'.

Students who had been living with foster carers were often driven by car to university and helped to settle into their new quarters. Those who were living independently had to manage by themselves. One young man described his feeling of acute loneliness when he saw other first year students and their parents unloading computers, television sets and crockery from the family car. He had travelled to the university by public transport with no one to accompany him.

Some students, especially in Cohort 1, missed the chance to obtain university accommodation because their local authority did not inform them in time about funding of rent payments. Demands for deposits or advance payment of hall fees also caused problems. In some cases students were eligible for hardship loans or grants from the college or university but were too disorientated to apply by the closing date. They had usually not received any advice on these matters from the local authority and felt overwhelmed by the deluge of information on all kinds of subjects that descended on them from the university. Some thought they could have absorbed it better if it had been given verbally or more gradually:

> *There is information given but there is not enough time for it to be read . . . they give you all these documents, all this paperwork as soon as you start university. The only time you have got to read it is two days before you have got to start your lessons on Monday. You start thinking about your coursework and you forget about the paperwork that has been given to you . . . the information I have got [about financial entitlement] I have got from you lot – coming to meetings and hearing from other students. [Now] I am the person passing some of this on to my mates who don't know what is going on.*

(Kameron)

SETTLING IN

During this early period many of the young people were heavily dependent on former foster carers, relatives or friends from home for emotional support and many of them went home every weekend even when they could not really afford the travel costs. One student always missed lectures on Monday mornings as a result of staying Sunday nights at home with her boy friend, and never really caught up in that subject.

One or two never quite made the transition from home. Louise did very well to get a place on an extremely competitive course at a top university. She enjoyed the academic side but felt out of place in the very middle-class student body and missed home acutely. At the end of the year she decided to transfer to a less prestigious university nearer home and went back to live with her former foster family. This was an exception however. By the second term most of the students had made new friends and were enjoying an active social scene.

MOVING TOWARDS INDEPENDENCE

About a quarter of the participants had already been living independently before they started university, but those who had been in foster placements or, in one case, a children's home, found they had a lot to learn. They counted that as one of the benefits of having a bridging period as a student before moving altogether into the adult world.

> *I've grown up. You're sort of flung into a situation where you've got to be independent. Also apart from the uni aspect, there's the financial aspect, where you're budgeting aren't you? You're trying to think about your money, you've got to think about your work, about feeding yourself, about not just uni work but also I had a part-time job so I was having to think about that as well, and organise time aside to do that. So I would say it made me more independent. I'm probably more grown up than some of my friends who are back at home, who've lived at home. At the end of the day I've got my own flat and they're still living with mum and dad and they've probably never done the washing or ironing themselves, or cooked for themselves, or all these basic things that you need to learn. I'd say I've learnt all that.*

MAKING FRIENDS

Making friends was crucial to their adjustment to student life. Participants who lived at a distance and had long journeys between home and university or who had caring responsibilities that prevented them from socialising could become isolated and much more vulnerable to dropping out if they ran into difficulties. Bernadette, for example, only had one close friend who she had known already before going to university. All those who had lived in university accommodation during their first year were emphatically in favour of it.

Some participants remained attached to former boy or girl friends and occasionally decided to go on living with them. This could sometimes be a source of stability and reassurance, as well as financial support, but it usually prevented the student from participating fully in university life. If the relationship broke up the student could be left in serious difficulties, as in the case of Serena, described in the next chapter.

Friends became increasingly important over the course of the three years and were almost always named as a significant source of support.

SOMEWHERE TO STAY

The students who had fewest problems were those who had a successful final foster placement which continued to provide a secure base during their time at university. A typical pattern was to spend the first year in hall and move in the second year to a shared house or flat. Sometimes this might carry on into a third year although not necessarily with all the same people sharing. When it worked well the housemates often became close friends and remained in touch after the end of the course.

Some participants were in serious difficulties when their former foster carers, who might be living on low incomes, took on new foster children and no longer had space for them to stay for more than the odd night.

> Sunisa was very close to her foster mother, whom she referred to as 'Mum', but her foster parents divorced during her first summer vacation and the family home was sold. She applied to the council for housing and was allocated a flat:
>
> *It was quite hard because I was just given the keys, and the flat was really, really bad and nothing was working, and the council was just like 'here's the keys, here's some vouchers for decoration, now beat it' – that was their kind of attitude.*
>
> It was only by going to the Children's Rights Officer that she managed to get essential repairs done and obtain equipment and materials to redecorate the flat herself. In retrospect she felt pleased with the way she had handled this situation:
>
> *. . . that experience helped me to grow up a lot more because I did it in a mature way. I went about it the right way and got a really good result.*

Some of the students we visited had good council accommodation, but often they were allocated flats in poor condition in very run-down areas. One young woman, homeless over the Christmas vacation, was sent to a bare flat infested with rats and had to sleep on a friend's floor. Problems also arose for many students as a result of failures of communication between social services and housing departments. It seems that neither had taken on the principles of corporate parenting.

> Kameron was constantly threatened with eviction because his rent was supposed to be paid direct but the payments never arrived on time. He came home from university one dark evening to find his flat bolted up with steel shutters. It took him a week to persuade the housing department that it was another part of their own authority that they should be pursuing for arrears of rent. He was not able to get any help from the Social Services Department.

Living alone in a council flat could be very lonely, and if it was not near the university travel time and costs often limited access to facilities and social opportunities. People in this position were particularly vulnerable and some reported having experienced serious depression.

WORK AND PLAY One of the longer-term objectives of the *By Degrees* project was to enable students to 'get the most from their time at university'. We therefore asked participants about their involvement in aspects of university life outside the formal academic programme. Over half of the first cohort said they could not afford to belong to any clubs or societies or go to plays, films or concerts. There was a higher participation rate in Cohorts 2 and 3, of whom 43 per cent belonged to at least one university organisation and ten people were members of committees or took on leading roles. A few went on sponsored trips or expeditions, some of them helped by grants from the Frank Buttle Trust. Recreation for other students consisted of visiting friends or going out for a drink. One young woman said, 'We got really poor towards the end so it was pretty much just hanging out.'

Paid work Available employment tended to be in supermarkets at weekends or pubs and bars in the evenings, so that those who had to work during term time not only had a restricted social life but often found it difficult to spend as much time on personal academic work as was needed, with the result that their grades suffered. One participant was at an Oxford college which prohibited students from taking jobs during term, but most universities seemed to take the view that it was up to students to decide how much paid work they could cope with. Vacations were taken up with working for money to pay off or reduce overdrafts. It was a matter of concern that so few managed to get a holiday during the entire three years, even in the second summer vacation when most of them were badly in need of a break.

FINANCIAL MATTERS

It is often pointed out that all students from less affluent families are likely to be short of money and some have to rely on the student loan and whatever jobs they can find to support themselves. However, unless they are estranged from their family, students who have not been in care often have the benefit of substantial hidden subsidies even if they get no regular contribution. They can probably go home for a few days any time they like without being expected to pay and are unlikely to return to university without a bag of groceries and household goods. If they run into accommodation difficulties between one year and the next they are still likely to have somewhere to go.

For students who have been in care the position is very different and their entire experience of university is strongly coloured by how much financial support they receive from their local authority (Figure 5.1). As a minimum some local authorities paid tuition fees and the Care Leaver's Grant,[1] and expected students to survive by taking out the full student loan and working to make up the shortfall. Others paid rent in full or in part as well as making a variety of other payments, for example for books, and equipment and travel. Some students received a monthly or fortnightly payment to cover all expenses throughout the year. Rent might be included in this or paid separately. In addition to payments from the local authority a few students were successful in obtaining loans and grants from their HEI. Some participants received a Leaving Care grant of up to £1000 paid in instalments, but others received nothing at all.

Students who were eligible (they had to have started their courses before they were 21) also received grants from the Frank Buttle Trust. Some told us that they could not have continued at university without this help. The criteria for awarding grants were quite stringent and all applicants were expected to have taken out the maximum student loan, so the fact that over half were assessed as needing grant-aid in Cohort 1 compared with only 26 per cent in Cohort 3 indicates that the level of local authority funding had improved. A small proportion of students also received financial help from birth and/or carer families and from other charities, as shown in Figure 5.2.

Figure 5.1: Financial support received from local authority

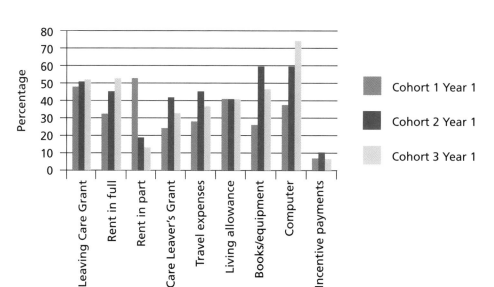

Figure 5.2: Financial support from other sources

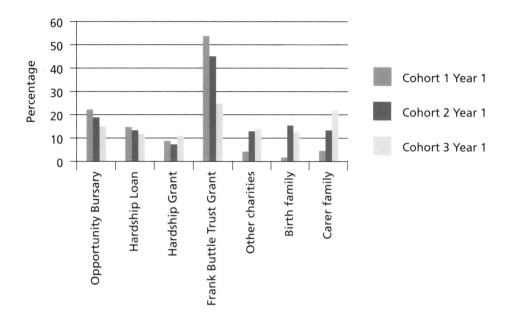

Debt and fear of debt

Some care leavers who had volunteered to take part in the project decided not to go on to university because they were afraid of ending up with an unmanageable level of debt at the end of their course. One young woman who was living with an elderly foster carer was discouraged from taking up her place because her foster carer did not understand that all students are now expected to finance their university courses by taking out loans. The foster carer believed that any form of debt was to be avoided at all costs.

Most participants took out the maximum student loan by the end of three years and many also had bank overdrafts up to the limit, which was usually between £2000 and £3000. The average debt after three years for students in Cohort 1 was £11,235 compared with a national figure of £9,210, but many students owed much more, in one case over £20,000. Only one local authority made a contribution to paying off the debt when the student graduated, although this is a common practice for parents who have the means to do so.

RELATIONSHIPS

During their time at university participants were often juggling with complex networks of relationships: parents, grandparents, step-parents, siblings, step-siblings, foster carers and their children, social workers, house-mates as well as boy and girl friends. As noted earlier, many of their birth families were extremely volatile and a crisis might blow up at any moment. During the first year this was likely to throw the student off balance and disrupt their work pattern and living arrangements. By the third year they had often learned to distance themselves from family members who made excessive emotional demands. However, 58 per cent of Cohort 2 participants and three-quarters of those in Cohort 3 had continuing contact with at least one birth relative.

Celia's university life was overshadowed by chronic anxiety about her mother's repeated suicide attempts. In her first year she was constantly rushing home following every incident. Eventually she came to accept that there was nothing she could do about it and achieved a degree of emotional detachment that enabled her to get on with her own life. However, she continued to suffer from depression and failed her final year assignments. Earlier in the year she had received a letter from social services to say they could no longer provide her with a personal adviser, and this added to her feeling of abandonment:

I could have gone back. I was still debating it over the summer, but I knew deep down I didn't want to. The subject wasn't right for me and I seemed to have lost all motivation.

Last time we spoke to her Celia was working as a waitress.

Several respondents told us how much they had learnt about people from living in shared student houses.

Benita had a difficult time in her second year when she was deceived by a hard luck story into offering a room in her house to a student who she did not know very well. This young woman had frequent disputes with the other three tenants and refused to pay her share of the bills or help with the housework. Eventually they had to ask her to leave, which Benita found painful and upsetting since she felt responsible for the trouble. She said she would be much more cautious in future about taking people at face value.

One young man remarked that the ideal combination was two men and two women since the women tended to keep the house in reasonable order while having at least one man prevented the girls from being bitchy towards each other. There is clearly an element of stereotyping here, but he claimed that his observation was based both on personal experience and observation of other sharing arrangements.

ACADEMIC ISSUES   Students who had taken a year out before starting their course often found the adjustment back to academic work quite difficult.

Bernadette became pregnant in her last year at college and decided not to take up her place at a top university but to change to a less prestigious institution and start a year later.

All the whole year I was just focusing on my child, all the whole year I was like breastfeeding, washing baby, changing baby's nappies . . . I think that made me like forget even to hold a pen. When I started uni I could not do it for long, my fingers were aching, I could only do it for ten minutes.

Once at university she made a conscious decision not to participate in social or recreational activities but to concentrate 100 per cent on her child and her studies. During her course she never went out in the evening or at weekends. She estimated that in addition to lectures and seminars she spent at least 25 hours a week studying and working on assignments, more in her final year. Despite numerous practical problems she passed all her assessed modules and exams first time and plans to continue into postgraduate social work training.

Nearly all of the students said they wished they had worked harder in their first year. Not having much idea what to expect, they were often lulled into a sense of false security by knowing that marks in the first year would not count towards their degree and by the lack of overt pressure. In retrospect they realised that this was the time when they should have been learning the tools of the academic trade and that more effort at this stage would have avoided the problems they ran into later as the work became more demanding and assignment deadlines loomed.

Arthur enjoyed his first year immensely, but he still had a lot of growing up to do. He failed one module, which he put down to missing a crucial lecture due to oversleeping. In his second year, living in a shared house instead of a university hall of residence, he managed a better balance between academic work and social life, went on a 'brilliant' field trip and immersed himself in his subject, environmental studies. He found the third year dissertation very demanding and felt that he would not have passed without a great deal of help from his tutor, who happened to be the Head of Department. Like several other students he attributed some of his difficulties to interruptions in his early schooling due to his mother's mental illness and many different placements. Nevertheless he achieved his ambition to get an upper second and plans to do a higher degree after a year travelling.

Possibly because they were having more of a struggle with social relationships and sometimes with problems in their birth or foster families back home, many of the *By Degrees* students took quite a long time to become fully engaged with their degree subjects. In the first two interviews they often seemed more concerned with other matters. This had usually changed by the end of their second year, when many of them had developed a genuine enthusiasm for academic study and an interest in their subject for its own sake, not simply as a route to a good job. In one or two cases they pushed themselves too hard and immersed themselves in work to the exclusion of all else, and sometimes to the detriment of their health, but generally they managed to achieve a reasonable balance.

After the Christmas break in the third year course assignments and exam revision took over entirely. The final Easter vacation was the only one in which almost nobody took a paid job. There was a high drop-out rate from Cohort 1 in the first year which is discussed further in the next chapter, and many of those who stayed on obviously had a struggle. A high proportion had to do resits or resubmissions or had to stay on an extra year to retake modules. Figure 5.3 shows the outcomes for Cohort 1 at the time of the final interviews.

Of those who had completed their courses by December 2004, seven people achieved an upper second, seven a lower second, one person a third and one failed. The remainder were either on four-year courses or still completing outstanding modules.

The reasons given by students for having to do resits and resubmissions were:

- earlier deficiencies in schooling, literacy and numeracy problems
- difficulties in adjustment during their first year
- being overstressed by financial and personal worries
- leaving assignments to the last moment
- not spending enough time preparing or revising for exams (sometimes due to working long hours in low-paid jobs).

Twelve people dropped out over the three years, as discussed in the next chapter, but the rest seemed determined to continue. One student who dropped out in his first year started a new course at a different university two years later.

Figure 5.3: Cohort 1: outcomes after three years

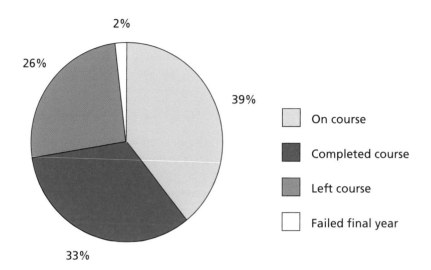

LOOKING BACK

In our final interviews with participants in the first cohort we asked them to reflect on their whole university experience. This might be very different depending on the type of course they were doing, where they lived in relation to the university and how much support they received from their local authority. However, they were unanimous in feeling that they had got a great deal out of continuing into higher education and that as a result they were much better off than other care leavers.

> *I would advise anyone to go to university. It's fun for starters, and academic-wise you upgrade your class. When it comes to thinking you have got that bit of you whereby you develop more than if you had never been to university . . . you are a step ahead, experience-wise, personal responsibility. You don't have anybody telling you that you need to go to university . . . it's up to you to get up out of bed and be committed to this.*
> (Eddie)

> *. . . You meet more intelligent people, some lecturers that when you do have a lecture with them they really, really open your mind to the issues and stuff like that. So from what I have learnt for the past three years at uni that has definitely opened me up a lot and made me more aware of a lot of things going on and changed my views. And you know it just broadens your horizons . . . so that's what my experience at university has done for me, just opened up more doors for my intelligence to be processing things.*
> (Barbara)

Many of the students remarked how much they had grown up and that being at university had enabled them to acquire social skills and learn how to assess other people: Eddie said that by the end he was one of the most popular people in his year. He described himself as choosing his friends carefully and 'making sure that the right people were around me'. He had excellent support from his local authority – 'I couldn't ask for better' – graduated with an upper second and now has a job as an advertising sales executive.

KEY FINDINGS

- Most participants greatly enjoyed their time at university and felt it had given them an opportunity to mature and acquire social and life skills.
- Some students did not get enough information before they started their courses and missed opportunities to apply for grants or obtain university accommodation. All students who had lived in university accommodation during their first year were emphatically in favour of it.
- Making friends was very important, both for emotional support and arranging second year accommodation.
- Council flats were of variable quality and there were failures of communication between housing and social services departments.
- Students who did not receive enough financial support from their local authority often took on too much paid work to the detriment of their academic progress.
- Lack of money also limited their social life and prevented them from engaging fully in university life.
- Several students said they could not have continued at university without grant aid from the Frank Buttle Trust.
- The average debt on graduation was £11,235 compared with a national figure of £9,210, but one owed over £20,000.

NOTE

1. The Care Leaver's Grant is funding to help with accommodation costs in the long vacation. Those eligible are full-time students in care on their sixteenth birthday and for at least three months afterwards and under 21 years at the start of their course. Young people receive up to £100 a week from the LEA, or it may be paid direct to the person supplying accommodation.

   It should not be confused with the Leaving Care Grant, sometimes called a Setting Up Home allowance. This is for all care leavers moving into their own accommodation. A social worker or adviser will assess the needs of the young person and apply for a grant for them depending on individual circumstances. It is usually not given as a lump sum but in the form of payments for different household items. There is no fixed amount. A total of around £1000 seems to be fairly typical but some of the *By Degrees* participants received nothing.

6 *Dropping out or hanging on*

The young people who volunteered to take part in the *By Degrees* project had originally shown themselves to be exceptionally resilient by getting to the point of being offered a university place after having spent at least part of their childhood in public care. However, resilience is not an absolute quality. The myth of the invulnerable child who can survive any adversity has long since been discredited (Kirby and Fraser 1997). It seems that tackling problems and setbacks can to some extent strengthen the ability to overcome a poor start in life, but each additional negative factor reduces the chances of continuing to do well. When we look at how the young people in the three cohorts coped with the stress of university life we see this clearly.

We identified seven main sources of stress:

- shortage of money
- fear of debt
- psychological problems arising from care and pre-care experiences
- difficulty with academic work, sometimes attributable to gaps in early schooling
- relationship difficulties with other students, boy or girl friends
- problems in birth or foster family
- isolation and lack of emotional support.

Of these, the first applied to nearly all our participants, even those who were relatively well funded by their local authority. Many also had problems in one or two of the other areas. It was when several of these factors coincided that they ran the highest risk of giving up the struggle.

FALLING AT THE FIRST FENCE

Several young people who volunteered to take part in the *By Degrees* project never made it to university. There were three main reasons for this. Some did not obtain the required grades and there was no one available to advise them either to apply for admission through clearing, or to retake their examinations. Some decided they were not yet ready to go to university, one was offered a promotion in his vacation job with a higher salary and better prospects and was unable to resist the temptation. A common reason, however, was that their local authority would give them no guarantee of financial support or accommodation during vacations and they believed there was a risk that they might find themselves destitute and homeless. On the other hand if they decided not to go to university or college they might be offered a council tenancy and a Leaving Care Grant which could appear misleadingly generous.

In any case, taking up a university place often seemed a risky business, especially if, in addition to financial worries, the prospective student had doubts about their ability to cope with the academic work or living independently. Personal factors, such as feelings of responsibility towards partners or relatives, also played a part.

Henry did well at school and was offered a place to read international relations at a leading university. Partly because he was urged to do so by his girl friend's parents, and against the advice of his foster carers, he decided instead to accept a post as manager of the shoe shop where he had worked during school holidays. Although he was paid a good salary and had no financial worries, it was a decision that he bitterly regretted by the time he was interviewed. He thought he might have made a different decision if he had had a chance to discuss the matter with a careers adviser or after care worker.

Those who were afraid to take up their university place because of uncertainty about how they would support themselves were mostly, though not exclusively, in the first cohort, before the CLCA was implemented. Their fears may or may not have been justified but usually they lacked any informed person who could have advised them.

DROPPING OUT

Of particular interest to the study were students who decided to leave university before finishing their courses. Given their achievement in entering higher education from care, their inability to complete their degrees was a particularly sad waste of potential that might negatively affect their future opportunities. In some cases it happened when the student was quite near the end of the course when it seemed the cumulative pressures simply became too much for them and they felt they had no alternative but to opt out. Researchers resisted, at times with difficulty, the temptation to take on a counselling role, but always urged the young person to contact the Frank Buttle Trust caseworker for advice before taking any irrevocable step. Unfortunately by that time the relief of having made a decision and the resulting reduction of stress usually prevented them from changing their minds or seeking a different solution.

Figure 6.1 compares the outcomes for the three cohorts after their first year in higher education. Altogether 12 students in Cohort 1 left university before completing their courses, although one of these started a new degree course after a two-year break. Three students in Cohort 2 left in the first two years and one in Cohort 3 in his first year. Three students moved to a different university and five changed their course without moving. Two students had to retake their first year and one failed her final year and decided not to retake the year.

Although the reasons for giving up courses were diverse, many could be attributed to a lack of adequate support. The constant anxiety of trying to manage on too little money, though not a concern exclusive to ex-care students, was far worse for them when there was no family to fall back on. On the whole, debt was a less common problem than we had expected. Student loans and bank overdrafts were a normal expectation and most participants seemed to take a responsible attitude to credit cards, only using them for a specific purpose such as taking advantage of the opportunity for a field trip or a holiday. In some circumstances, however, debts could get out of control.

Serena achieved a long-held ambition to read law in one of the highest-rated departments in the country, but decided to set up house with a boy friend instead of accepting the place she was offered in a hall of residence. At the time she was first interviewed she was enjoying her course and coping well with her heavy workload, but when the relationship broke up she was left in severe difficulty. She took on three part-time jobs in an attempt to pay off bank loans and credit cards and found it increasingly difficult to keep up with her university work.

It was very hard, an uphill struggle. Because I was living in a flat quite far out of the city I wasn't part of the university social life. It was just work and study and coming home in the evening to domestic work.

Trying to study while maintaining a household on a low income put a severe strain on students because they were having to think about all kinds of financial and practical matters alongside their academic work. But another problem, as for Serena, was that it set up expectations that were in conflict with the student role. Although living with a partner might provide stability and emotional support that was helpful, young people were sometimes seduced into aspiring to a suburban life-style that they could not afford, buying furniture, domestic appliances or other goods on mail order or credit cards.

Those who lived by themselves, on the other hand, could experience extreme loneliness. There was a clear consensus in all three cohorts that the best arrangement was to live in a hall of residence for the first year and, having made friends, to move into a shared house or flat for the second and third year. Those who maintained their tenancy for two successive years solved the problem of accommodation over the second summer (provided they could pay the rent). Others preferred to go back to former foster carers. But not everyone had this possibility.

Figure 6.1: Outcomes after first year for all cohorts

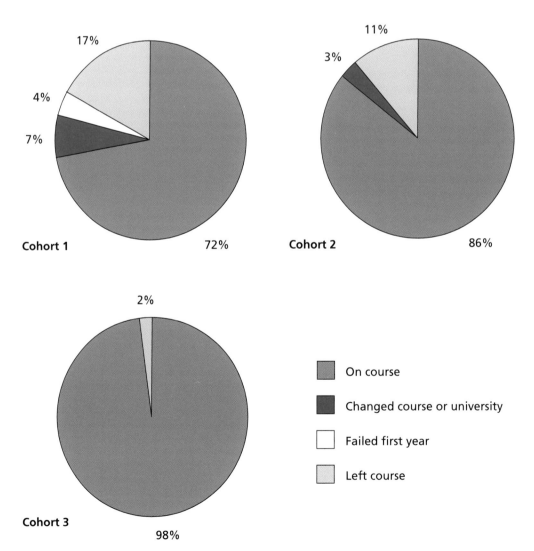

Travel problems

Some students committed themselves to long journeys in order not to lose their council tenancies, and in the end were defeated by the stress of daily travel and the isolation this caused due to not being able to participate in student social life.

> Mario asked to come into care to escape severe physical abuse by his father. Because he was already aged 15 he was placed in a young people's hostel where the environment was not at all conducive to study. In the middle of his A-level course he was allocated a council flat, one floor of a three-storey house. He was hoping to qualify as an aeronautical engineer and accepted a place at a college some distance from London but was unwilling to give up his flat, which he described as 'the biggest thing in my life – not to have to go back to the hostel'. He enjoyed the course and did reasonably well in his first year, but decided that he could not face another year of up to three hours travel a day, compounded by the unreliability of public transport which meant that he was constantly late for lectures.

Mario's case illustrates the impact of multiple pressures. Perhaps he might have persevered with his course, as other students with equally long journeys did. But at the same time he was having to fight a court case to remain in his flat when a bureaucratic muddle resulted in his rent not being paid, he had a struggle to meet assignment deadlines, and halfway through the year his parents, who had been married for over 20 years, split up without warning. His father moved abroad, leaving him as the main source of support for his mother and sisters.

Academic difficulties

In a few cases the gaps in early schooling seemed to catch up with the students as academic pressure and the demands of coursework mounted. At many universities the workload in the first year is quite light but increases rapidly in subsequent years. Typically, the third year includes a dissertation of between six and ten thousand words, and this often seemed to be a test too far.

> Boris obtained top grades for his practical assignments in applied art but found the written work progressively harder and gave up in despair a few months before the end of his course.
> Like a number of other students, he was on a course that offered a Higher National Diploma after two years, with an option to go on for a further year for a degree. Many who had originally intended to do this found the combination of academic and financial stress too great and decided to opt for the lower level qualification and find a paid job as quickly as possible. This was not necessarily a disaster. Boris's portfolio was good enough to get him a rewarding job in his chosen field where he was much happier than persisting in what he felt was a vain attempt to meet the standard for written assignments.

There was also a small group of young people who did not complete their university course because of caring responsibilities. Three female students were looking after a child, and struggled to arrange adequate childcare (although others managed to combine study and parenthood successfully). One young woman decided to give up full-time study in order to care for her boy friend who had been involved in a serious accident, with the intention of going back to university once he was well enough.

Mona decided to leave her course because she repeatedly failed assignments, not through lack of ability but because she did not understand what was being asked of her and could get no help from a tutor. As she put it, 'I felt that I was flogging a dead horse.' After working in a bank for a few weeks she decided to move to London and describes her situation as 'really close to being homeless'. She was fortunate in finding a job as an assistant in a publishing firm and a room in a shared flat but still regretted not having made the most of her opportunities. Asked what would make her happy she replied, 'Doing something that I can be proud of again, like I used to. I haven't had that for such a long time.' She had made the decision to leave university on her own, having no chance to talk it over with anyone older or more knowledgeable than herself. She particularly resented her inability to make contact with anyone from her local authority and their lack of interest in her. She expressed the view of many other participants when she said:

> *Considering the fact that I was under a court order for all that time and they don't even know if I'm still alive, I think it's really off – I think it's terrible that they haven't checked up on me or anything.*

Mona's advice to other care leavers starting at university was:

> *Don't throw it away. Don't be stupid . . . Even though it seems like a hard time, three years out of your life is nothing compared to a lifetime struggle without a degree.*

The effects of earlier experiences

Another important cause of dropping out can probably be traced back to the individual's family and care history, and this is something that makes them particularly vulnerable compared with other students. As we showed in Chapter 3, the majority of the participants had experienced extremely traumatic experiences within their birth families, and sometimes also while in care. Problems sometimes manifested themselves as a difficulty in concentration or persistence. Dean, for example, suffered many years of abuse from his stepmother before eventually running away from home and coming into care. He had not seen his birth mother since the age of three. Despite this, he passed ten GCSE subjects, four of them with high grades. However, after a few weeks at university he dropped out of his course, rejecting the advice of his grandmother who had strongly encouraged him to go in the first place.

Most of those who dropped out had endured severe physical, sexual or emotional abuse during childhood. While these experiences tended to be relegated to the backs of their minds while they were in the relatively protected environment of school and foster home, once out on their own intrusive thoughts could resurface. At university, these young people often reported difficulty in forming new relationships and could find themselves quite isolated emotionally. Some told us that they experienced flashbacks or periods of severe depression. This could happen unpredictably so that they found themselves unable to study for long periods, and sometimes were unable to ask for help. Once they failed to submit assignments on time the work piled up into what they saw as an impossible load. Having nowhere to turn for advice or support, running away from the problem seemed the only solution.

In some cases students in this position were advised to suspend their studies with a view to returning later. For home-based young people this is often a good idea. They will usually have parents supporting them who will keep their longer-term goal of going back to university firmly in view. However, for students without family backing this is risky as, especially if they manage to obtain a job that pays reasonably well, the idea of going back to poverty and academic pressure can seem too daunting. Two students who were advised to take time out during a period of particular difficulty did manage to return after a break – one had a very supportive foster family and the other moved back with his birth family – but usually sticking it out was a more successful option.

Few of our participants found Student Support Services in their institution helpful and some had had no contact with personal tutors. For these young people the only available source of help when something went seriously wrong was the Social Services Department. Yet, accessing such support was by no means straightforward and often caused intense frustration, as Francesca told us:

> *I had no clue and I didn't know how to get into contact with them ever, so I would never know who to speak to to ask for help . . . They started off by making a verbal agreement that they would be in touch once a month and it wasn't. It wasn't even once every six months. It was just like, well, never . . .*

Although once the CLCA was implemented this type of situation should have occurred less often, there were reportedly many cases where the student's named after-care worker or personal adviser had moved on without a successor being appointed. In one case the whole department had moved to a new address without informing the student. This falling off of contact particularly affected students in their third year when social services departments and after-care teams seemed to take the view that students should need less support, being older and more experienced. In fact the reverse was true. Because of the much greater academic demands of the third year and the build up of anxiety about debt, this was the time when many young people were in particular need of an informed and sympathetic adult to listen to their problems and offer helpful advice.

Perhaps social services cannot be held entirely to blame. One problem that particularly affects young people who have been in care is their reluctance to ask for help, or even to recognise that they need it. The phenomenon of 'pseudo self-reliance' is characteristic of those whose basic needs have not been met in early childhood, which was the case for many of those in our research sample. One young woman put it succinctly when asked what was her main source of support. She answered, 'me, myself and I'.

HANGING ON Many of the students had been through times when they felt overwhelmed and seriously considered dropping out but had managed to work through their problems or find help. We asked participants if there was ever a time when everything could have gone wrong and what had enabled them to carry on.

> After a difficult start Sandra felt that her third year was going really well until she developed health problems and was diagnosed with a serious chronic condition.
>
> > *I did think that maybe I wouldn't be able to get through the year because . . . you get to a point where you just want to stop fighting sometimes and it was so difficult to get up and get on with my work. Because whenever I ached or I would get pains it puts you off eating and you think 'maybe I just want to go home and let mum and dad look after me'. But it was, well this is what I have always wanted to do and so there is no point quitting now because I am so near the end.*
>
> Despite her medical condition she graduated with an upper second in history and went on to study for a higher degree. Her main support came from her foster parents and boy friend but she also thought being willing to talk about her problems had helped her to come through.
>
> > *The main thing is that if you do have any problems don't be afraid to see somebody about it because, as I found, it means they can help you and it makes you feel so relieved that you have shared the weight of it.*

There were a number of other participants with health problems, both physical and mental, which made life hard for them. Six people in the first cohort had chronic health conditions, such as asthma, heart and stomach problems, and one young woman had 60 per cent hearing loss in one ear.

At first it seemed that there were few mental health problems, but as the interviews progressed these became increasingly evident. Some participants had received counselling when in care and were referred for further counselling at various points during their time at university. Two students suffered from severe depression: one had to suspend her studies and the other failed her final year and decided not to retake it.

Overcoming disability

There was only one participant in the study who was registered as disabled. He needed exceptional determination to access higher education and persist in the face of the many obstacles he encountered.

Adam was born with cerebral palsy and taken into care when his mother was diagnosed with a serious mental illness. He went through several placements before eventually moving to live with his grandmother and unmarried aunt, which gave him a secure base and a quiet and supportive environment.

It was one of his earlier foster carers who recognised his ability and fought to have him transferred to a mainstream school. Despite missing many months of school due to repeated hospital admissions for operations to improve his mobility, he obtained eight GCSEs with A–C grades, a GNVQ with Distinction, and was offered a university place to study computing.

Once at university he found it very difficult to obtain the services to which he knew he was entitled. It took several months to sort out matters such as getting books out of the library, a notetaker for lectures, and transport from home to university. He became very anxious about falling behind with his work and failing to meet deadlines. Although his Disabled Student Allowance covered his living expenses so that he did not have financial worries, many people would have given up in the face of the practical problems he had to overcome. However, far from giving up, he became an active campaigner on behalf of disabled students and expects to complete his degree successfully.

Considering the many problems they had to face it is perhaps more remarkable that such a high proportion of our participants managed to complete their courses than that some of them left prematurely. It is encouraging that the drop-out rate was considerably lower for Cohorts 2 and 3. Only one Cohort 3 student decided to leave in the first year compared with eight in Cohort 1, which perhaps reflects better support from local authorities following implementation of the CLCA.

KEY
FINDINGS

- Some participants never got started because they did not achieve the required grades and no one was available to advise them.
- The drop-out rate for *By Degrees* participants was 10 per cent compared with the national average of 14 per cent.
- Fewer students left prematurely from the second and third cohorts.
- Students were most vulnerable to dropping out when they experienced three or more stress factors.
- Some young people who have been in care are reluctant to ask for help, or even to recognise that they need it.
- Those who lived a long way from the university, either to keep council tenancies or to stay with partners, were cut off from social life.
- Academic difficulties, especially with mathematical subjects, often resulted from deficiencies in earlier schooling.
- Participants with problems did not get appropriate help from Student Support Services in their institution and many had no contact with personal tutors.
- Difficulties in contacting social services caused extreme frustration.
- Students with dependants struggled to obtain adequate support even when it had been promised before they started their courses.
- One severely disabled student had great difficulty in obtaining the facilities he needed but persisted with his studies.
- There was a serious lack of appropriate help for mental health problems.

7 Coming from overseas

One of the most interesting features of the research was the increasing numbers of participants from overseas, many of whom had come to the UK as unaccompanied asylum-seekers. As the research progressed it became evident that they differed from the rest of the participants in terms of past experience, reasons for entering local authority care, their perspective on life and perception of education.

Young people coming from other countries made up almost a third of the overall research sample. The age at which they arrived in the UK varied, with some having lived in their birth countries only in the first year or two of their lives. However, the largest single group had come to England as adolescents.

In the first cohort just under 20 per cent were born overseas. In the second cohort this rose to 30 per cent and in the third cohort to 41 per cent, reflecting the rise in the number of people seeking asylum in the UK during 2001 to 2003. This compares with only 5 per cent of asylum-seekers in the care population as a whole. The majority of overseas young people participating in the research were Black African (69 per cent), originating from East and West African countries such as Uganda, Ghana, Nigeria and Ethiopia. There were also participants from China, Sri Lanka, Kosovo, Turkey and other European countries.

In contrast to the overall sample the gender distribution was more evenly balanced, and among those who came to the country as unaccompanied asylum-seekers it was reversed, with 62 per cent male and only 38 per cent female. This corresponds quite closely to the national figures, which show that in 2004 70 per cent of looked after asylum-seeking children were male (DfES 2005).

COMING TO THE UK Some of the young people came to England to join parents or other family members already living and working in the UK. Others were escaping political or religious persecution and the decision to leave sometimes had to be made very suddenly. Most participants came to the UK, with hopes of a better life for different reasons, but the circumstances under which they arrived were usually traumatic. The young person was often not consulted. Damian told us:

> *I didn't know I was coming to England. I was at school. I was studying at junior high school. I was picked up from school saying, 'You're going to join your mum.' And I did ask, 'Why all of a sudden?' . . . I was picked up from school. And I went back home. Got a few things. And then I moved to England. I mean, personally, I didn't really want to move.*

> Tai made the decision himself to leave his family and start a new life away from the civil unrest in his own country. He spent five days in the back of a lorry in cramped conditions, crossing many countries to get to England. On arrival he was dropped off at midnight in what he later discovered to be Hyde Park, not knowing where he was, what to do or where to go.

Some of the young people travelled with friends or 'agents' employed by their families to escort them and were extremely vulnerable to exploitation. They were not in a position to question the motives of their escorts, who were often pursuing their own interests, because, as Marilyn said, 'when you're trusting someone who's meant to be helping you to improve your life you don't really ask much'.

> Marilyn took the opportunity to come to England with a family friend who promised that she could look after his children and study. However, on arrival she was taken to a house where several other girls were staying and it soon became clear to her that the girls were being used for prostitution. She managed to escape from the house and found her way into local authority care with the assistance of Spanish-speaking strangers who she approached in the street.

> Marko's family was in grave danger for political reasons and an agent was paid by a friend to travel with him to England. After two nights in a bed and breakfast in south London, Marko awoke to find himself alone, without money or identification. The agent had taken all his possessions and disappeared, leaving him with the bill to pay for the room. Fortunately the landlord was sympathetic and gave him his bus fare and directions to the Social Services Department. Stories like these were common.

ATTITUDES TO EDUCATION

Whatever their previous experiences almost all of the participants from overseas had in common an intense drive to pursue their educational goals. Some had come to the UK explicitly for that purpose. When Sue was asked why she and her sisters had decided to leave Uganda her reply was simply, 'to come to university'. Some of these young people had endured extraordinary privations and we could only wonder how they had the emotional and physical strength to integrate into a new society with limited knowledge of the country and often lacking basic proficiency in the English language. We were struck by the way they made the most of any resources available in a way that some indigenous young people do not.

> Muddah was born in Africa and escorted to England at the age of 14 by a friend of the family to escape danger in his country. His escort left him to fend for himself and he found his way to a local hospital from which he was taken into care. He had three foster placements and took the initiative himself to ask for a move from the first two because they showed no interest in his education. His third placement he described as 'perfect'. Here, he felt welcomed and part of the family. His foster carers strongly supported his educational ambitions, their own children having gone through further and higher education. At the time of interview, Muddah was undertaking a marketing course at university. The financial package he received met the majority of his needs, and he had a good support network made up of friends, his social worker and his faith in the Muslim religion. However, he struggled with the academic work and attributed this to not having developed a routine of studying while in his two earlier foster placements.

> Guyenne as a young boy was caught up in the Rwandan conflict and had spent three years with his sister in a refugee camp before coming to the UK, speaking no English. As his sister, the only other member of his family to survive the massacre, was older than him, they were put in a council flat. His sister was so severely traumatised that, aged 14, he had to undertake all domestic responsibilities. He decided to concentrate entirely on learning the language for a whole year and then went on to take GCSE and A levels. At the time of interview he was doing well in the second year of his law course, at a good university, living with his sister in an immaculately kept terraced house. Unusually, he had negotiated, with the help of a sympathetic social worker, to be allocated accommodation near the university of his choice rather than within his care authority.

It was common to hear overseas participants speak of education as a passport to a better life, and they were much more likely than UK-born young people to say that their parents had strongly encouraged them to work hard in school. This seemed to be a key factor in their determination to succeed. Asked if her parents had taken an interest in her education Toni said:

> *Yes, very much. She [birth mother] always said the only thing you have is education, you have to learn. She would always emphasise that she would be very disappointed in us if we didn't go to school and get good grades and that kind of thing. I think she regretted the fact that she didn't go to school herself.*

When Sue, the daughter of a politician, was asked how she came to put such importance on education she said:

> *[when she was young] You were just going to school because your parents were telling you to go. But when I go to secondary school I started to realise that it was important to be educated. That is when I started analysing what I wanted to be and what I wanted to do when I grow up and things like that.*

Overseas participants generally came from families with somewhat higher educational qualifications and occupational backgrounds compared to UK-born care leavers in the study. Direct comparisons can be misleading because in many of the countries from which participants came education, if available, had to be paid for – even completing elementary school could not be taken for granted. Also, many of our respondents, especially the home students, had limited knowledge of their parents' education or even what jobs they did. However, for Cohorts 2 and 3, which had the most overseas participants, we compared the highest level of education reached by either parent and found a considerable difference as Figures 7.1 and 7.2 show.

There were also significant differences in occupational status between the birth parents of UK and overseas students, especially at the lower end. A much higher percentage of UK-born parents were unemployed or in occupations classified as 'elementary', such as factory workers, drivers, car park attendants or school dinner assistants.[1]

OVERSEAS PARTICIPANTS AT UNIVERSITY

Once they achieved their ambition to go to university there was often not much to differentiate the overseas students from the others. There was some evidence, however, that they retained a clearer focus on their educational goals and were more determined to do well academically, partly because they felt they were fulfilling their parents' ambitions as well as their own:

Being able to get this far is the greatest, and it's everyone's dream to have his son or his daughter at university level. That is the only thing that parents could give to a son or a daughter, is education. And the biggest dream is to see them graduating from university.

This contrasts with what we were told about their motivation by many of the UK-born participants, who were more likely to say that their driving force was to pursue a different way of life from that of their parents or to disprove the predictions of people who had underestimated their ability.

Some of the overseas students, like Bernadette, whose story is told in Chapter 5, made a conscious decision to focus entirely on their studies at the expense of any kind of recreation or social life. One young refugee from China was living at the top of a tower block in an outer suburb of London, travelling an hour each way to university. He worked through every weekend to support himself, determined to achieve his ambition of becoming an architect.

Overseas students reported spending many more hours a week on private study, in addition to lectures and seminars, than UK-born students. Although numbers were too small for statistical significance, nearly a third spent 20 or more hours a week on personal academic work, as against 6 per cent of home students. We asked all of the students to rate their academic performance compared with that of their peers. Most thought they were doing about as well as other students but among overseas students 32 per cent assessed themselves as doing better than average, compared with only 18 per cent of UK participants.

Figure 7.1: Overseas and UK participants: birth mother's education

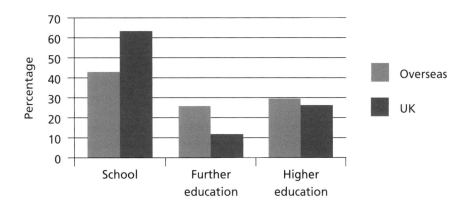

Figure 7.2: Overseas and UK participants: birth father's education

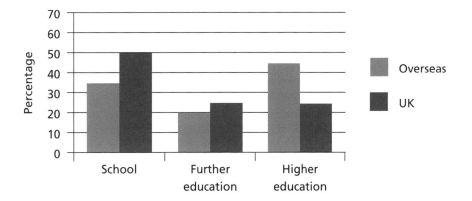

Simon thought it was important to balance work with other interests. He believes in having fun. Even though he has a difficult daily journey he plays competitive badminton, loves dancing, listens critically to music, and is passionately interested in films. Looking back, Simon reflected how he had changed since he first went to university:

It was an excitement because it was something I wanted to do. I knew it was a big struggle before I went, but I was really excited about it. When I got into it I understood that it wasn't just about excitement . . . I had to put in lots of hard work to see that I get my degree . . . It has made me more of a responsible person and it has made me see further and higher . . . I feel I can achieve more than what I have already achieved, which I think is quite good.

Simon's long-term ambition is to become a United Nations mediator.

SEEKING ASYLUM

Coming to the UK is only the beginning of a long journey towards naturalisation and enough stability for the young people to achieve their educational aspirations. This path is often blighted by the insecurity surrounding their status and possible repatriation to their homeland. In addition they have to cope with the emotional pain of not knowing what has happened to the family they left behind. Sometimes they broke down in tears in speaking of them.

Many young people seeking asylum live in limbo, not knowing what will happen to them, while at the same time trying to establish some sort of foundation for everyday living. As part of the research process we tried to identify the status of overseas participants. Even gathering clarification of the different terms from the Home Office was a difficult task owing to rapid changes in government policy under political pressure. The categories we originally used – exceptional leave to remain, indefinite leave to remain and full refugee status – had already changed by the time of writing. Exceptional leave to remain has been replaced by Humanitarian Protection and Discretionary Leave and refers to those awaiting status of refugee, provided their application has not already been refused. Twenty-eight per cent of our overseas students across all cohorts had both full refugee status and indefinite leave to remain and the remainder are still awaiting status decisions.

Students were well aware of the vulnerability of their situation – two-thirds of all applications for asylum were refused in 2002 and since then the policy has become much tougher. Some of the students in this position suffered immense stress under the imminent threat of deportation and it is remarkable that only one dropped out. In fact, of the overseas students only four dropped out over the life of the project, all from the first cohort.

We were greatly impressed by the resourcefulness and resilience of many of these young people, particularly the asylum-seekers. Unfortunately not many of them experienced sensitive support from social workers of the kind described by Ravi Kohli (2000), and it seemed perverse that those who were doing well in higher education and were on course to make a valuable contribution to society, either in the UK or in their country of origin, lived in constant fear of having their studies brought to an abrupt end.

Kiernan was the youngest of three, brought up in a loving, supportive family where education was given the utmost importance. The day the troops swarmed into his hometown, his life changed forever. In desperately trying to seek help Kiernan was separated from his family. The Red Cross has not been able to locate them and it is not known if they are alive or dead.

Kiernan endured an eight-day trip hidden inside a lorry, escaping from the war-torn streets of Pristina where he had been sleeping rough, dodging bullets. Aged 15, he was left alone by the side of a road just outside London.

Kiernan did not have a good experience of care. He was moved time and again, including one move in the middle of his GCSE exams. In one placement he was robbed of the few possessions he had managed to gather. In another, drug dealing and outbreaks of fighting were the norm. Through all this he sustained his ambition to go to university, passed all his first year exams and was on the point of starting his second year when he was suddenly summoned to an interview with the Home Office at the other end of the country. No one was available to accompany him from his leaving care team and he had no legal representation. The decision to reject his application to remain in the UK was left on his answer phone. The prospect of being returned terrifies him; he still suffers from anxiety attacks and relives the trauma from his past. He has no family or friends in Kosovo, no possibility of continuing his education, and will once again find himself completely alone in the world.

One of the researchers attended to support him in his appeal. This time he did have legal representation, but of very poor quality, and at the time of going to press, we heard that the appeal had been rejected.

Although the overall number of people seeking asylum in the UK has dropped substantially over the past two years, unaccompanied children (under 18) are disproportionately concentrated in a small number of London boroughs. The problems this creates for the local authorities are discussed in the next chapter.

KEY FINDINGS

- Sixteen per cent of the research sample came to the UK as unaccompanied refugees compared with only 5 per cent of the care population.
- In the third cohort 41 per cent of participants were born overseas.
- Some young people travelled with paid agents who quickly deserted them, leaving them vulnerable to exploitation.
- Birth parents of overseas participants were more likely than those of UK students to have higher education and less likely to be in unskilled occupations.
- Almost all of the overseas participants were strongly motivated to pursue their educational goals and especially to go to university.
- Once at university overseas students put in twice as many hours of private study as home students.
- Seventy-two per cent of asylum-seeking students were awaiting status decisions and feared repatriation. In some cases they received very inadequate support from their local authorities.

NOTE 1. According to *Standard Occupational Classification* (US Department of Labor 2000).

8 The local authority as corporate parent

As Sir William Utting pointed out in his first report, *Children in the Public Care* (1991) there is no way that a public institution can reproduce the unconditional love and commitment that most parents offer their children. So the widely used term 'corporate parenting' is to some extent a contradiction, especially as it confuses three different functions (Jackson and Sachdev 2001). On the other hand it can provide a useful benchmark against which to assess the performance of a local authority.

In one sense corporate parenting refers to the duty of all departments of a local authority to cooperate in promoting the welfare of children and young people who are separated from their birth parents. In another sense it refers to the need to coordinate the activities of the many different professionals and carers who may be involved in the child's life. This is the job of the social worker. The third sense shifts the emphasis from 'corporate' to 'parenting', which we defined in our interim report as 'the performance of all the actions necessary to promote and support the physical, emotional, social and cognitive development of a child from infancy to adulthood' (Jackson *et al.* 2003: 56). This function is delegated by the local authority to those providing day-to-day care for the child, overseen by the social worker.

In numerous pronouncements, notably in launching the *Quality Protects* programme (Department of Health 1998) in England, the Government has admitted that the parenting of children in public care has been deficient, particularly in relation to their education, and has led to poor outcomes and diminished life chances. Accepting responsibility may be the first step to change. But how much responsibility should fall on a local authority and how long should it continue? How should it balance the allocation of resources between children who have been looked after for many years against the claims of those who only come into care towards the end of their childhood? Should young people coming from overseas have equal rights with those born and brought up in the UK? The CLCA attempts to answer some of these questions, but in practice each authority has to interpret it in the light of its own priorities and local conditions.

PROVISIONS OF THE CLCA

The Act sets out the duties of the local authority towards four categories of children and young people aged 16 and over who are or have been in care:

1. 'eligible children' aged 16 and 17 who are still in care
2. 'relevant children' who have been looked after for at least 13 weeks but have left care
3. 'formerly relevant children' over 18 who have been in either of the previous two categories
4. 'qualifying children over 16'.

The local authority is responsible for keeping in touch with young people who have left care and for providing support for those in education or training up to the age of 24.

One of the key requirements of the Act is the need for the local authority to provide young people, foster carers and staff with clear information about financial allowances, entitlements and any conditions attached to them. The authority is required to develop a specific higher education financial protocol. The protocol should set out clearly the availability of:

- financial support during term time for university students
- financial support during Christmas and Easter vacations
- payments for foster carers if they are able to offer formerly fostered young people the opportunity to return to them during vacations
- support to enable young people to apply for university bursaries, access funds, student loans and tuition fee exemption.

It seems to be assumed that students will work to support themselves over the summer vacation but they may also be eligible for a Care Leaver's Grant from the LEA, as explained in Chapter 5.

Young people over 18 cannot legally be 'fostered' but there is provision for extending foster placements in cases of need (for instance if the young person is assessed as vulnerable or requires continued support to complete further or higher education) or for converting foster placements to supported lodgings. The local authority can continue to pay the same allowance as before or, more commonly, a reduced rate.

Under the Children Act 1989 the local authority already had powers to provide financial assistance in relation to higher education, but the CLCA converts these powers into duties. The local authority must provide accommodation in vacations, assistance with educational expenses and a range of other payments according to circumstances, either directly or through former foster carers.

The Guidance to the Act states:

> *It is important that young people are clear about the funding duties owed to them by their responsible authority, and about what the authority would normally expect to provide funds for.*

It adds a crucial caveat:

> *It is also self evident that the authority operates within limited resources and that there will from time to time be competing demands on those resources from different children, and that they may not always be able to fully meet those demands.*
>
> (DfES 2003c: 9.5)

In practice this enables local authorities to conform to the *minimum* requirements of the CLCA while differing substantially in the level of support they offer to ex-care students.

HOW FAR HAS THE CLCA CHANGED LOCAL AUTHORITY POLICY AND PRACTICE?

The fact that the first *By Degrees* cohort started their university courses before the Act was implemented enabled us to establish a baseline from which to compare changes over time and to assess their impact on students. Twelve local authorities were selected to form a core group and all but one were visited yearly to track developments. The selection, as explained earlier, was based on percentages of looked after children obtaining five or more GCSEs at grades A*–C and produced a good spread of inner and outer London authorities, metropolitan boroughs and shire counties. The people nominated to take part in the interviews were a very diverse group, including leaving care team leaders, project managers, social workers, coordinators for training, education and employment, housing workers and careers advisers.

The same basic questions were asked at each interview, with some additional questions in subsequent discussions. The first interview helped us to establish what local issues were likely to affect the implementation of the CLCA, the second was designed to identify targets and chart progress over the following year, and the third focused on the future of educational provision for care leavers after the end of ring-fenced *Quality Protects* funding, and also asked to what extent ongoing dissemination of findings from the *By Degrees* project had influenced practice.

To complement the core group study we carried out two surveys of English local authorities in the first and last year of the research. In the autumn of 2001 we carried out a survey of all local authorities in England. It requested descriptive and statistical information on available services for young people in and leaving care who planned to enter further or higher education. Sixty-three local authorities returned the questionnaires after several mailings and reminders by telephone and email. We found that there were big differences between authorities and that despite having been given over a year to plan implementation progress was very slow. No one person seemed to have the information to complete the questionnaire in full, with the result that there was much missing data. It was often difficult to distinguish between willingness to provide particular forms of support in theory and what students actually received.

Perhaps the most important finding at this stage was that fewer than half of those who responded had any agreed policy on support for young people from care entering higher education. Three-quarters claimed to have a system for keeping in touch with students at university and to allocate workers to provide continuing personal and emotional support, but this did not agree with what we heard from our participants.

Overall the Act was welcomed and it was thought that it would help to provide a more uniform service.

> *The tone was set by the Frank Dobson letter,[1] which highlights the fact that it is a corporate responsibility, and ultimately the legislation gives people in social services the clout to argue for support for young people.*
>
> (After-care manager, north-western authority)

The top five most common forms of financial and practical support given to care leavers accessing higher education were Care Leaver's Grant, provision of vacation accommodation, expenses for educational equipment, one-off payments for special circumstances and travel expenses. Fewer than half of local authorities provided computers or retainers to foster carers for vacation accommodation.

Some authorities offered imaginative forms of educational support beyond standard expectations and responded helpfully to individual requests. For example, a Midlands authority provided allowances and travelling expenses for religious festivals and holidays, another paid medical costs not covered by the NHS, for instance for complementary medicine treatments. One authority paid for personal tutoring in the run up to examinations and offered rewards for individual achievement. Some offered assistance with applications to charities and help with graduation costs. One paid air fares for a student taking a year out. Of course there may have been many others that provided payments of this kind, unknown to the person who completed the questionnaire.

When asked about what they felt was the most important aspect of the CLCA at the point of implementation, the majority of those who replied took a very positive view, responding that it was having a clear statutory responsibility to finance and support students until the end of their course. They did, however, foresee many difficulties, especially around their capacity to provide the level of financial support that would be required and securing vacation accommodation in areas of housing shortage. One respondent thought that it would be difficult to develop an 'aspirational culture' among all agencies and individuals involved in working with young people in and leaving care. Another predicted that keeping in touch with some young people might be hard if they felt they had had enough of the care system. On the other hand maintaining the commitment to continued contact and support might require more staff resources than were available.

Findings from the second survey

Three years later we conducted another postal survey of all local authorities in England including the Scilly Isles. The aim was to assess the extent of policy and practice development since implementation of the CLCA. The response rate (29 per cent) was disappointing despite numerous repeated mailings and reminders (see Table 8.1). Fifty-nine per cent of replies came from authorities that had responded to the first survey. It was only possible to make direct comparisons between those who completed questionnaires on both occasions, although we also drew on information from authorities that took part in the second survey only. Detailed findings from the first survey can be found in our interim report (Jackson *et al.* 2003).

It was not always clear how to interpret the information provided by respondents. Some local authorities give much more generous living allowances than others, expecting them to cover all anticipated expenses, such as stationery, clothing and travel, whereas others, which offer lower allowances, may pay rent direct or give grants for specific requirements which add up to a similar level of support in total.

As can be seen from Figure 8.1 some aspects of the comparison give grounds for optimism. Importantly, more authorities are providing retainers to former foster carers during vacation

Table 8.1: Local authorities responding to *By Degrees* surveys by region

	Responding (%)		
	First time only	Second time only	Both times
North	33	39	32
Midlands	16	6	12
East	9	–	8
London	20	11	32
South	22	44	16
Total	100 (N = 69)	100 (N = 17)	100 (N = 25)

Figure 8.1: Local authority provision before and after implementation of the CLCA

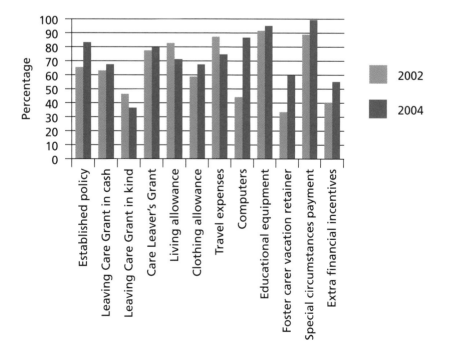

periods and a higher proportion now have agreed policies relating to provision for care leavers entering further or higher education. In some cases this meant formalising previously existing practices but the fact that they are now written down and publicly available to young people, carers and social workers represents a significant advance. The proportion of authorities providing computers has almost doubled, and this finding was confirmed by differences between the three cohorts of participants. Those in Cohort 3 were much more likely to be given laptops when they started their courses, whereas Cohort 1 participants either received computers very belatedly or not at all.

DISPARITIES BETWEEN LOCAL AUTHORITIES

Despite the provisions of the CLCA there are still considerable differences between levels of support provided by different local authorities, and even within the same authority. This has major implications for the young people concerned in terms of experience and outcomes. In our interim report we told the story of Samantha and Celia, two young women doing similar courses at the same university, in care with the same authority but different social services teams. Samantha received excellent financial and personal support throughout her course, including a regular vacation job in the council offices, was able to take a full part in university life, and graduated with a good degree and no need to retake any exams or assignments. Celia, by contrast, was entirely dependent on her student loan and what she could scrape together by working in pubs and restaurants through every vacation as well as in term time. By her third year she was completely worn out. She described herself as depressed and demotivated, and when she failed her finals refused the chance to retake her third year.

The second survey showed more local authorities having clear written policies regarding support for care leavers in higher education so that anomalies such as described above are less likely. However, the level of support available from different authorities and in different parts of the country continues to vary widely, as the comparison in Table 8.2 shows.

We also asked what additional assistance could be given under Section 24 of the Act. Authority A offered a financial reward for A-level passes, bursaries of £1750 to undertake work participation, Leader of the Council grants for holiday projects, driving lessons, an official Letter of Congratulation, a start-up pack for new university entrants, and an established practice of employing graduates who had been looked after by the authority. Authority B admitted to having very limited arrangements for support of young people in higher education but cited as an example of their willingness to assist that they had just awarded a £100 book grant to a care leaver. The respondent recognised the need for policy development in this area.

A positive change that emerged from both the second survey and the core group interviews was increasing awareness that local authorities should be taking an active role in encouraging young people in care to aim for university. Joint working and early planning were seen as key areas, encouraging young people, social workers and foster carers to place education high on the agenda.

Those authorities who were more advanced in their thinking stressed the importance of schools and social services working together to provide a seamless transition for young people embarking on higher education courses. They recognised that personal, emotional, academic and financial support were all essential, as well as ensuring that information about provision was transparent and accessible to all potential students and those working with them. An emerging development was the increased number of compacts between local authorities, schools, colleges and universities which, even if not targeted specifically at care leavers, have the potential to increase their participation in higher education.

Table 8.2: Comparison of support provided by two authorities

	Authority A (South East)	Authority B (North West)
Transport/travel expenses	In part to and from university	
	In full to and from home	No
Rent paid	In part	No
Vacation accommodation Grant	In full	In full
Holiday allowance	Yes	No
Graduation allowance	Yes	No
Living/maintenance allowance	Yes	No
Expenses for educational equipment	In part	No
Extra financial incentives	Yes	No
One-off payments for special circumstances	Yes	Yes
Leaving Care Grant (mostly in cash)	Yes	No
Leaving Care Grant (mostly in kind)	Yes	Yes
Retainers to foster carers for vacation accommodation	Yes	No
Clothing allowance	Yes	No
Provision of computers/ access to computers	In part	No
Established policy on financial support	Yes	Yes
Number of young people in higher education at the time	2	1

ASYLUM-SEEKERS An issue that came increasingly to the fore in the course of the project was the greatly increased number of young people, usually aged between 14 and 17, who arrived in England unaccompanied, or who were abandoned by the adult who came with them. This was a particular problem for local authorities in coastal areas and some London boroughs. One authority reported that 75 per cent of their care leavers came into this category. A very much higher proportion of these young people aspired to a university education compared with UK-born children in care, which had important implications for local authority budgets if they were to be given the same opportunities as other children, as required by the Guidance to the CLCA.

Many of these potential high achievers needed additional language support and tuition, and because of fragmented earlier education might have to do a foundation course instead of embarking immediately on a degree, meaning that they would require an additional year's funding. Frequently changing and increasingly punitive asylum and immigration regulations cut across the CLCA and may often work against its aims. When budgets were tight questions might be raised about eligibility. A leaving care manager from an authority in the North East told us, 'Sometimes I have to fight corners to get people to understand why young people should be financially supported.'

It is worth reiterating here that not only had many of these young people survived unimaginably traumatic experiences, but the majority of them were exceptionally determined and hard working. They seemed on course to make a valuable contribution to society, either in the UK or, as some of them told us, by returning to work in their countries of origin once the political situation had stabilised.

SUSTAINING SUPPORT

Our later interviews with Cohort 1 and 2 research participants confirmed the doubts expressed by respondents to the first local authority survey about keeping in touch with students throughout their course. The students reported a serious falling off of interest in their progress and sometimes difficulties in obtaining agreed financial contributions during the second and third years. Fewer than 20 per cent had continued contact with a named personal adviser or after care worker during their third year, although this was a time when increasing academic pressure and financial problems meant that they might be in particular need of support. Even those who could turn to former foster carers and had a good circle of friends seemed to feel the want of concern from their local authority and to have a sense of being abandoned, like Mona, quoted in Chapter 6.

Many of them commented that it was strange that social services departments, having invested so much in their education, were so indifferent to what happened to them. They would have liked to receive the occasional friendly telephone call instead of contact only occurring when they made a request (and sometimes not even then). Perhaps some after care workers are unduly worried about being seen as intrusive. Growing competence and independence, however welcome, do not necessarily signal a wish to cut off former relationships.

There is a useful analogy to be made here with the behaviour of ordinary parents of university students, who expect fewer visits home and less frequent phone calls as the years go by, but continue to be strongly interested in the experiences of their children and would be greatly concerned if they lost contact with them.

THE CONTRIBUTION OF *BY DEGREES*

Some of the respondents to the postal surveys as well as those interviewed for the core group study commented on the usefulness of the project in raising their awareness and drawing attention to the range of support needed by young people in higher education. They felt it had stimulated them to ask questions about monitoring progress on implementation of the Act and how they should be helping ex-care students. In later interviews respondents remarked that the information contained in the interim report had provided a baseline and a clearer framework within which to develop their services. The Frank Buttle Trust benchmark figures (see Appendix 5) were considered particularly useful. One respondent said that participating in the project had given her the confidence and information she needed to take matters to senior management when she thought young people in her authority were not getting the support to which they were entitled.

KEY
FINDINGS

- The Guidance to the CLCA (DfES 2003c) includes a let-out clause so that in practice local authorities differ very widely in the level of support that they provide.
- The *By Degrees* project raised awareness within local authorities of the range of support needed by young people in higher education.
- In 2004 many more local authorities than in 2001 had an agreed policy on support for care leavers going to university.
- The proportion providing computers doubled between the two *By Degrees* surveys. More students in Cohort 3 received adequate financial support than in Cohort 1.
- Few local authorities were able to provide continuing personal support throughout the three years. Young people often said they felt abandoned and had great difficulty contacting anyone for help when they ran into difficulties.
- The growing number of unaccompanied asylum-seeking children created resource problems for some authorities.

NOTE

1. When launching the *Quality Protects* programme (Department of Health 1998), Frank Dobson, then Secretary of State for Health, wrote personally to every elected member emphasising the responsibility of the whole local authority to promote the education of looked after children.

9 Widening participation

THE POLICY
CONTEXT

Soon after the start of the *By Degrees* project the Government announced a new initiative, the Excellence Challenge, to increase the number of people from disadvantaged backgrounds who could benefit from higher education. This was launched in September 2001 with ring-fenced funding of £190 million. The widening participation agenda gained increasing momentum throughout the life of the project, and one aim of the research was to find out how far this extended to young people who had been in care.

The initiative was later extended to 2006 while the Government's White Paper *The Future of Higher Education* (DfES 2003d) signalled the commitment to bring together the Excellence Challenge, renamed *Aimhigher*, and the *Aimhigher Partnerships for Progress*. The purpose of the joint initiative was to establish a national outreach programme to support a range of activities including collaborative working between schools, colleges and HEIs in order to increase the aspirations and educational attainment of young people from disadvantaged backgrounds.

For the year 2004 to 2005, £272.6 million pounds was allocated for the Government's widening participation initiative through the Higher Education Funding Council for England (HEFCE). The money has two main aims: pre-application costs for outreach programmes and post-application costs such as for covering institutions for recruiting students who are more likely to drop out and for funding Opportunity Bursaries. There is also an allocation of 4 per cent for students with disabilities. The allocation of funding is determined on the basis of the number of students who complete their year of study, thus giving HEIs a financial incentive not only to encourage recruitment of students from areas and families with no tradition of participation, but also to prevent them from dropping out. In fact 78 per cent of the funding is to improve retention of students.

A further strand of the Government's widening participation programme consisted of setting up the Office for Fair Access (OFFA). All publicly funded providers of higher education in England who decide to charge tuition fees above the standard level are required to submit an access agreement to OFFA. This should set out how they will safeguard and promote fair access for under-represented and low income groups – through bursaries and other financial support and outreach work. Although care leavers are not specifically mentioned there is clearly potential for them to benefit from these arrangements.

THE *BY DEGREES*
SURVEYS

At an early stage in the project we wrote to all vice-chancellors of universities in England and all heads of Oxford and Cambridge colleges to ask if they had any policies to encourage care leavers to apply and what arrangements existed for any necessary support. Replies were received from 96 HEIs. The great majority had not previously been aware of care leavers as a group with particular needs and circumstances. The findings from this inquiry are reported in detail in our interim report (Jackson *et al.* 2003).

We repeated the exercise three and a half years later, but by this time almost all institutions had appointed staff members with specific responsibility for widening participation of disadvantaged groups, so it seemed appropriate to address the questionnaire to them, this time including institutions in Wales, Scotland and Northern Ireland. Surprisingly, the response rate to the second survey was much lower and most of the answers were fairly brief. The majority of completed questionnaires were from 'old' institutions, that is, those that had the status of university before the provisions of the Further and Higher Education Act 1992 came into force.[1]

RAISING ASPIRATIONS

Following on from the widening participation initiatives, the majority of universities had plans, if not processes in place, to encourage applications from candidates with disadvantaged backgrounds. For the most part, these were based on guidelines from the *Aimhigher* programme and involved practical outreach initiatives such as summer schools, visits to schools by university staff and student mentors in schools.

When asked whether the university has plans to build links with schools and colleges while especially encouraging children and young people in care to aim for higher education, they tended to use the umbrella initiative of widening participation and young people from a disadvantaged background rather than those specifically from care. However, one HEI in the South West encourages schools and colleges to include looked after children in their widening participation cohorts and a university in the South East runs outreach programmes with local authorities specifically to encourage young people from care to aim for higher education.

ADMISSIONS PROCEDURES

Out of those who responded to the second survey, 77 per cent did not keep any record of which students have a care background. Three institutions said that, if known, this information would be kept on file, but they were only likely to be aware that the student had been in care if he or she was also a recipient of specific funding. Only one of the universities stated that there was an agreed policy regarding care leavers. Reasons given for the lack of any specific policies were that the number of applicants who had been in care was too small to justify any special efforts, and unless they chose to disclose the information their care background would not be known.

Some universities take account of young people's backgrounds in the admissions process. Passing summer schools can lead to unconditional offers at a university in Wales. In one institution in the East Midlands widening participation is an integral part of the training of admissions tutors. A London university has been running a scheme for the past two years whereby 'widening participation' applicants (of which care leavers are one group) are encouraged to submit an additional information form with their UCAS application. The information provided can lead to the candidate being made a lower offer for a particular course, although not below the minimum offer for acceptance by the university. Four institutions will lower entry requirements, accept alternative qualifications in place of A levels or give credit for experience, indicating a potential to succeed.

An institution in the North East has been running a programme to encourage progression from state schools and colleges in the surrounding region. The programme offers activities to raise aspirations and provide evidence of potential, with an alternative entry route via an Assessed Summer School. It targets those young people in state schools from socio-economic groups 3 and 4 and with other disadvantage factors such as coming from neighbourhoods where higher education participation is low. Successful completion of the summer school can lead to conditional offers for A levels at a slightly reduced level (for example BBB instead of AAA) or vocational qualifications. Seventy schools and colleges are currently participating in this programme.

There are also compact schemes between universities and schools and colleges whereby points can be awarded to the student (equivalent to 40–60 UCAS points) for involvement in a range of activities beyond the purely academic.

The great majority of HEIs, however, still do not have application procedures that highlight care leavers as a discrete group. We found no evidence that this is likely to change since few described plans for the future. Some respondents considered it inconceivable that someone who had been in care could possibly reach the standard required for entrance to their institution. Occasionally their comments revealed considerable ignorance of the care system, for example assuming that all children looked after by local authorities are in children's homes:

It is essential that the educational provision for those in residential care improves significantly before we will be able to take more students from this background.

A more sympathetic response from an equally prestigious university was:

The key bottle-neck here is their educational attainment. It is a tragedy that so many children in care are so poorly educated. We can certainly make allowances here, but our courses are highly demanding and we can only go so far in this regard.

We should point out that all the *By Degrees* participants had obtained offers of university places on their own merits and several of them told us very emphatically that they would not have wanted to be treated differently because they had been in care. Some had academic records that would have enabled them to apply to far higher-ranking institutions than the ones they actually attended. Low expectations and lack of access to informed advice limited opportunities as much or more than examination results.

FINANCIAL SUPPORT FROM THE HEI

The majority of institutions had no formal structures for supporting care leavers. Only one said there would be special provision of £300 from the government funds and bursaries for young people who had been looked after by local authorities. Three said care leavers are given priority when allocation of additional funds, such as the Access to Learning Fund, is considered. When care leavers are known, one institution makes sure the young person is aware of all support services and is receiving appropriate financial support. Thirty-three per cent said they provided no special financial support to care leavers. Whether this is purely due to lack of information on care leavers in their institutions is unclear. For those who said they would provide support if the student's ex-care status was known, this was from existing general funding and not from any fund earmarked for care leavers.

PASTORAL SUPPORT

Again, as with financial support, most pastoral support was not specific to care leavers. However, one university in the North East makes a point of encouraging known care leavers to take up university residence because it has full pastoral support on site. Another has a designated pastoral tutor who closely monitors the welfare of young people with a care background. However, the vast majority have no pastoral support scheme targeting care leavers and do not intend to plan any in the future.

STUDY SUPPORT

As with pastoral support, study support is not specific to students with a care background. Eighty-six per cent of the sample did not offer additional study support to known care leavers. Those who do provide this type of support for students do so by assessing need and running additional study groups and summer school programmes aimed at students who are under-performing. Only two institutions mentioned care leavers as a specific group in relation to study support. One college offers pre-entry summer schools with an emphasis on study skills. The other, a south coast university, provides welcome packs, inductions and publicity detailing available support for all students but is planning to include material targeted at care leavers through agreements with local authorities. Only one institution planned to provide specific study support to students with a care background in the future.

IMPROVING ACCESS AND RETENTION OF DISADVANTAGED YOUNG PEOPLE

Responses seemed to indicate a consensual support for developing services within the university to recruit and retain more young people from communities and families with little or no experience of higher education (which of course is a condition for charging maximum top-up fees). Most described their work under the Government's widening participation initiative. Those who are active in the area have links with schools and colleges and training programmes for admissions staff. A Scottish university told us that as a result of its schools and community outreach work, 10 per cent of its students now come from disadvantaged backgrounds.

By far the majority (95 per cent of those responding to the survey) had no policy specific to recruiting or retaining care leavers, nor any plans to develop one. Fourteen per cent of institutions did indicate an interest in reviewing their strategies in order to reach more disadvantaged young people, but with no particular focus on those who had been in care, even though they might be considered the most disadvantaged group of all. Many universities still take the view that young people with a care background could not possibly have the educational requirements to succeed in higher education. This is clearly mistaken. Over the course of the project the *By Degrees* participants attended 68 different HEIs, many of them top universities, as listed in Appendix 3.

The respondents seem to be misinterpreting the well-known fact that the educational attainment of looked after children is generally very poor to mean that no young person who has been in care has the ability to benefit from higher education. The *By Degrees* research has shown that this is quite untrue. However, some respondents made the valid point that universities are the last link in the educational chain and cannot be expected to make up for earlier deficiencies. Many of our participants did obtain excellent GCSE and A level grades, but this was often due to their own determination and persistence rather than good schooling opportunities. As we showed in Chapter 4, more than half went to secondary schools at the lower end of the league tables and there is ample evidence of past neglect and indifference to their educational progress within the care system (Borland *et al.* 1998; Jackson and Sachdev 2001).

LINKS WITH LOCAL AUTHORITIES

According to the survey, 23 per cent of HEIs had developed links with local authorities to varying degrees. One south coast university has had discussions highlighting the needs of particular disadvantaged groups, such as asylum-seekers, refugees and travellers as well as specific schools and communities, but not specifically care leavers. Another institution has set up links with the local Area Child Protection Committees and hopes this will help them introduce support earlier, although most children who are the subject of child protection procedures do not come into care (Gibbons *et al.* 1995).

Only three HEIs specifically mention young people with backgrounds in care. An institution in the East Midlands meets with social services and care teams with the aim of targeting young care leavers – they feel there is a lot of work to do. A university in the South East has mentoring schemes covering students in care in the surrounding county. A university in the region of Yorkshire and Humberside also provides mentors for a number of young people in care or at risk of coming into care.

FUTURE PLANS

Many HEIs responded sympathetically to our inquiries but said the problem was that they had no way of knowing if applicants or students had been in care. It is possible that more would develop appropriate policies if the information were routinely available: without it they cannot begin to provide the support that is often much needed. We had many discussions with young people on this point.

Some were quite definite that they wanted to leave their care background behind and make a fresh start when they began university. However, when we asked a simple question, 'Would you have ticked a box that you had been in care if there had been one available on the UCAS form?' 77 per cent, as mentioned previously, answered yes, although with some reservations. A few said they would want to know why the question was being asked and what services might be available as a result.

It seems that for the HEIs there is a tension between putting in place plans and strategies to improve access and retention of all students from disadvantaged backgrounds as opposed to targeting care leavers as a specifically needy group, which might carry a risk of stigmatisation. However, we would argue that students who have been in care have usually had experiences which mean that they may need additional support beyond what is provided for those who have at least had the advantage of growing up in their own families. Moreover, anything that is done to help ex-care students is also likely to benefit other students who come from low income families and poor communities by making the university authorities more aware of their difficulties.

One thing is clear: if we want more young people in care to continue into higher education there need to be stronger links between local authorities and universities. With widening participation officers appointed in most institutions, it should be possible to have a named contact person in each university for leaving care teams to get in touch with when one of the young people under their care starts university. Students may feel more comfortable about this if it is made clear that information regarding past care status is confidential, and some of the participants specified this as a condition of ticking the box on the UCAS form.

KEY FINDINGS	
	● The Government's widening participation agenda, aiming for more people from disadvantaged backgrounds to access higher education, provides an advantageous policy context for increasing numbers of care leavers going to university.
	● Only one university is known to have a comprehensive policy relating to care leavers.
	● Few universities have a policy of lowering admissions criteria for care leavers, so the *By Degrees* participants won places on their own merits.
	● Participants attended 68 different HEIs.
	● Seventy-eight per cent of *Aimhigher* funding is for retention of disadvantaged students but only three institutions considered providing special help for those who had been in care.
	● Various kinds of outreach programmes had developed between the first and second *By Degrees* surveys but only a few were specifically targeted at care leavers.
	● Ninety-five per cent of institutions do not offer any pastoral support to students known to have been in care.
	● Two institutions have plans to provide additional study support for care leavers; 86 per cent have no such plans.
	● Seventy-seven per cent of research participants said they would be prepared to tick a box on the UCAS form to indicate that they were care leavers.

NOTE   1. Some respondents stated that the information was given in confidence so no institutions are identified by name in this chapter.

⑩ Conclusions

Over the course of the *By Degrees* project we increasingly came to see the care leavers who volunteered to take part as collaborators in a shared enterprise. That is why throughout the report we have referred to the young people who travelled with us on this journey as participants rather than research subjects. We wanted to study their experiences from their own perspective, not to impose our ideas on them. They have a great deal to tell us, not only about what it is like to go to university from a care background but also about the care system itself, and we have tried to let their voices be heard. Our conclusions and recommendations are based as much on their ideas and suggestions as on our own observations.

WHAT DID THE PARTICIPANTS THINK OF THE *BY DEGREES* PROJECT?

In the final interviews, which took place in the autumn of 2004, we asked all the students about their experience of participating in the research and what they would like to be the legacy of the project. Individual participants had different levels of contact with members of the research team over the years. Some had been interviewed at length on four occasions and had used every opportunity to take part in focus groups, conferences and social gatherings. A few students who were seriously lacking in support from other sources telephoned frequently and had long conversations with the researchers. At the other extreme were some who were interviewed on one occasion and had no further contact.

We asked, 'How would you rate the way the *By Degrees* project has been carried out and your contacts with the research team?' By the end of the project we felt we had come to have a strong rapport with many of the participants, but we were still surprised by the warmth of their response. Some typical comments were:

> They [the researchers] have been fantastic; it's been carried out in a very very professional manner. And my contacts have always been superb.

> nothing less than exceptional . . . it's just been excellent. Too good to be true. I thank my social worker so much for putting it to me.

> It's been very professional . . . top notch! Thumbs up. I'd recommend it to a friend.

> I think it's been excellent, ten out of ten. I've had more contact with you than I probably got with my social worker when I was in care.

Some were aware that the researchers had undertaken long journeys to meet participants on their own territory:

> It's been really good. I've felt sorry for you having to lug around Britain! Having to walk down Mansfield Road in the pouring rain to meet me, having to drink out of a cup from a filthy kitchen.

All thought that the research had been carried out in a competent manner, and particularly appreciated the reliability of the researchers in always keeping appointments on time, returning telephone calls and being where they said they would be. They felt they had been treated with respect and fully consulted at every stage. Many of them contrasted this with previous experiences with social services.

Those who came to the social events were delighted to meet, usually for the first time, other university students who had been in care and to exchange experiences. The House of Lords celebration was, of course, a highlight and a few had felt almost overcome by the grandeur of the surroundings and finding themselves the centre of so much attention. The majority took it in their stride but said what a great occasion it was and how much they had enjoyed being taken on a tour of the House by Lord Laming.

The greatest benefit of taking part in the research, according to many respondents, was the opportunity it gave them to reflect on their experiences of care and education and to see them in a new light.

> *The conversations that I have with you, it sort of helped me to think back on what I've done. Stuff that I've achieved, or maybe stuff that I need to do, or stuff that I can improve on. The knowledge of other people in the same shoes as me. So partly I don't feel so alone.*
>
> (Noah)

Because being in care is a minority experience, young people do not compare themselves or assess their achievement in relation to others who are looked after, but in relation to their home-based peers. Most of them had no idea that, as care leavers, they were exceptional. Compared with other young people of their age their academic attainment was creditable but not outstanding. Few assessed their own performance as better than average. Finding out that they had done better than 99 out of 100 other care leavers was a considerable boost to their self-esteem.

> *I think it's made me appreciate what's happened to me and what I've experienced, given how few people end up going to uni after they've been in care. And it's just made me really proud of what I've done.*
>
> (Eddie)

> *In a way it makes me proud to realise [what I've achieved] . . . Because I always forget that I am someone who has come from a disadvantaged background. And it feels good to know that you can help people in the future as well.*
>
> (Sandra)

They had also found the process of responding to the researchers' questions had helped them to clarify their own ideas and consider alternative ways of dealing with problems and plan for the future. Although the researchers usually resisted the temptation to give advice, they could often suggest other sources of information and point people in the right direction, which again was found very helpful.

A few of the students were quite distressed at the prospect of the project coming to an end, so much had they appreciated their contacts with the research team. All were extremely keen that the results of the research should be widely known and that the message should get across to social workers, teachers and managers that far more children in care should be encouraged to aim for higher education and given the support they need to get there.

HOW TYPICAL WERE THE *BY DEGREES* PARTICIPANTS?

Statistically speaking it is probably harder for a young person who has been in care to access any form of higher education than for home-based children to get to Oxford or Cambridge. The life story interviews that we carried out with all participants did much to explain the low representation of ex-care students in the university population. We feel great admiration for the young people who had to overcome so many obstacles to reach university in the first place and continued to pursue their goals often in the face of continuing difficulties. Some of them displayed extraordinary resilience and determination.

But paradoxically, we were also struck by how ordinary they were, in the sense of being like other young people of the same age. As one participant said, 'I don't feel like I'm in care – I'm just a student like any other.' This is important because it suggests that improvements in policy and practice have the potential to enable a far greater number of young people in care to go to university than do so at present. We need to reject negative labels like 'damaged' that too often attach themselves to looked after children and focus instead on their capacity to recover and flourish even after the most horrific experiences.

Were there obvious differences in the backgrounds and characteristics of *By Degrees* participants and other young people in care? Every individual who took part in the study was different from every other, but only one group stood out as distinct within the whole research cohort: those who had come from overseas, in particular asylum-seekers, as discussed in Chapter 7. Otherwise the profile of the participants was quite similar to what is known of the care population generally. It seemed that they were slightly more likely to have better educated birth parents, or at least relatives who were concerned about their education, than other children in care, but we cannot be sure of this since there is no published evidence and we did not have a control group. Reasons for coming into care corresponded closely with those given in official statistics: various forms of abuse, mental and physical illness of parents, domestic violence and family breakdown were the most common factors.

From their own accounts some of the young people had been through periods when they had presented serious behaviour problems to schools and carers. On the whole, however, the *By Degrees* students had avoided coming into conflict with authorities. Suspensions and exclusions were rare and, once in care, very few, other than asylum-seekers, had been out of school for more than a few days at a time. The only thing that distinguished them from other looked after young people was that, despite extremely negative early experiences, their school performance was at an average level or above. Clearly personality factors and cognitive ability must have played some part in this but we have no evidence to suggest that the participants were exceptional. Again we draw the conclusion that the obstacles that prevent most children in care from realising their educational potential lie within the care and education systems and not in the young people themselves.

THE CONTRIBUTION OF THE CARE SYSTEM

It is easy to forget amid so much evidence of the shortcomings of public care that its purpose is to improve the lives of children and that in many cases it is successful. Some of the participants, especially those from overseas, had bad experiences of care placements, both in residential and foster care, but for the majority coming into care was a positive turning point. Often they regretted that it had not happened earlier. Most UK-born participants doubted that they would have got to university if they had remained with their birth families.

Residential care had provided a stabilising experience for one young woman, but there was no case where it had made a positive contribution to a young person's educational progress. It is a tragedy when a highly motivated young person who is doing well at school is placed in a home where noise and confusion make it impossible to study. Several participants told us that they had narrowly escaped being drawn into a culture of truancy, delinquency and drug misuse.

By contrast, the findings of this project demonstrate the capacity of high quality foster care to transform the educational opportunities of children who have had adverse early experiences. Many respondents had been falling behind at school until they were placed with foster carers who regarded education as very important, gave them strong support and encouragement, and provided a warm and affectionate home environment. But even when the relationship with foster carers was less than ideal, living in a foster family still seemed to provide a better background for educational success than either residential care or independent living.

Young people who had become well integrated into foster homes, often describing former carers as their 'real' family, continued to find them an invaluable source of support throughout their university career. It is important for local authorities to recognise this since they often have great difficulty in providing adequate personal and emotional support otherwise. A modest retainer enabling a foster carer to keep a room, or at least a bed, for the student in vacations is a very good investment.

There was no evidence from the participants' accounts that foster carers had been specially selected to improve their educational opportunities; this seemed to have happened largely by chance. We conclude that there is great, unrealised potential to use foster care as a key resource to raise the educational attainment of children and young people in care.

FINANCIAL AND PERSONAL SUPPORT FROM LOCAL AUTHORITIES

While the educational attainment of children in care continues to lag so far behind that of children in the general population, it might seem unreasonable to argue for more resources for the few who are already so much more successful than the majority. We believe that this is a very mistaken view. In the first place these young people surely deserve some recognition and reward for what is still an exceptional achievement. Secondly, if we genuinely wish to raise aspirations (which is a phrase that appears frequently in official documents) young people must have something to aspire to. Once it becomes a normal expectation for children in care to continue their education to 18 and beyond, and for many more to go to university, this will seem a reasonable goal for social workers and carers to propose to them. Moreover the best ambassadors for higher expectations are ex-care students who are enjoying their university experience and receiving good support from their local authorities.

As reported in Chapter 8, we found great variation in the level of support offered by different local authorities. Under the CLCA local authorities have a statutory duty to provide financial support and accommodation to young people who have been in their care up to the age of 24, but this was interpreted in widely different ways. In some cases promises of support given by one worker were disowned when that person moved on. Lack of resources was often given as the reason for failing to provide adequate funds for students or for cutting off payments to foster carers. However, it is noteworthy that on the whole the authorities that provided the best support were those who had most ex-care young people in higher education. This may have given them a more realistic idea of the costs involved, but they also tended to adopt a more systematic approach, sitting down with the student and working out exactly what was needed instead of pulling a figure out of the air.

Students are entitled to receive support from a personal adviser throughout their time at university, but in practice we found that this was very seldom available. Turnover of social work and after-care staff was partly responsible, but also the idea that by their third year young people should be fully independent. As we pointed out earlier, this is not the expectation of ordinary parents, and nor should it be of corporate parents. The third year of a degree course is a period of high stress. Although many young people can look for emotional support to their friends, when more serious problems arise they need to be able to turn to a supportive adult. In addition some ex-care students are more vulnerable because of their adverse early experiences.

PREVENTING DROP OUT

While the 10 per cent overall drop-out rate for *By Degrees* participants was lower than the national average of 14 per cent, reflecting the determination and persistence of the young people, almost every case represented a sad loss of potential. The marked differences between Cohort 1 and the two subsequent cohorts suggest a connection between the level of support provided to students and their ability to remain on course. Although surprisingly few cited money problems as the main reason for their decision to leave prematurely, there was no doubt from their case histories that constant financial worry was an important contributory factor. When local authorities failed to provide adequate payment for living costs and accommodation, students were liable to run into debt or to take on far too many hours of paid work to avoid it. Declining academic performance and increasing anxiety and depression often followed.

Following implementation of the CLCA local authorities were obliged to provide at least a minimum level of financial support. Indications from Cohorts 2 and 3 at the time of writing are that the final drop-out rate will be considerably lower than in Cohort 1. We therefore draw the conclusion that if local authorities want their high-achieving care leavers to complete their courses successfully they must budget to provide them with adequate support. According to most of the students who had graduated by the final interview, the Frank Buttle Trust benchmark figures given in Appendix 5 would have met their financial needs, but most had received considerably less.

Many students reported difficulty in obtaining informed advice when choosing courses and institutions or at critical moments such as when A level results were published. The majority were happy with their choice even though there was a strong element of chance about it, but those who drifted into courses to which they were unsuited or committed themselves to long journeys or uncongenial institutions regretted not having been better advised. The HEIs have an important role to play here, and the growth of compacts between colleges and universities and local authorities is an encouraging sign. However, as yet the strong policy steer from the Government on widening participation does not seem to have raised awareness of the particular needs of care leavers.

COULD MORE CHILDREN IN CARE GO TO UNIVERSITY?

This is part of a much larger question of how to improve the educational performance of looked after children generally. To increase the proportion of care leavers going to university we need to enable them to attain the examination success to make it possible and also to change expectations throughout the system. There is no shortage of information and guidance about how this can be done. Apart from official guidance and the recommendations contained in the Social Exclusion Unit report (SEU 2003), the Who Cares? Trust has produced a particularly useful set of materials called *Measuring Progress: Enabling children in care to fulfil their educational potential* (2004), and their previous Equal Chances programme, as well as the National Children's Bureau 'Taking Care of Education' project have developed many good ideas for helping children to do better at school.

Some children in care already do well at school but very few of them continue into higher education. We hope that this report has shown what young people with a care background can achieve when they are given a chance.

FUTURE RESEARCH

This first study of university students with a background in care has told us something about how a few individuals managed to overcome so many obstacles to reach, and in most cases succeed, in higher education, but not about how many others, perhaps equally able, failed to do so. In order to find out why, we would need to start further back, for example by identifying a group of young people in care at 15 who achieve similar good GCSE results, and compare those who go on to university and those who do not. Very little is known about the post-16 education of young people in care other than what has emerged from the present study, and this is an area where research is urgently needed.

Secondly, we note that the majority of local authorities have only one or two looked after children going to university each year, if any, but a few authorities have far more. Case studies of these authorities might provide valuable clues for their less successful neighbours.

Finally it is clear from our in-depth interviews that many of these young people, who might be considered the successes of the care system, continue to have severe unresolved psychological and emotional problems related to their family and care history. Much more research is needed into the most effective ways of helping them, and of course the many thousands of other young people who are prevented by similar problems from reaching their educational potential.

We will give the last word to one of our participants:

> *I would like to think that when the final report comes out it is actually used and listened to and that it does improve things for young people in the future. In particular that local authorities will look at it and won't immediately just say, 'well we haven't got the money so that's not possible,' but that the whole project can have its voice and achieve something.*

KEY FINDINGS

- The young people felt valued and respected throughout the project and this may have contributed to the relatively low drop-out rate.
- They appreciated the reliability of the researchers, in returning telephone calls and keeping appointments, in contrast with their previous encounters with social services.
- Discovering that they had done better than 99 out of 100 other care leavers gave a substantial boost to their self-esteem.
- A great benefit of taking part in the research was the chance it provided to reflect on their experiences of care and education.
- High quality foster care can transform educational opportunities for children who have suffered adverse early experiences, but there was no case where residential care had made a positive contribution.
- Local authorities who provided the most generous support were those who had most young people in higher education.
- All the *By Degrees* participants were keen that the results of the research should be widely known in order to raise expectations and enable more young people in care to go to university.

11 Recommendations

CENTRAL GOVERNMENT

1. The *Guidance to the Children (Leaving Care) Act 2000* (DfES 2003c) should be revised to make it clear that financial support from local authorities should not be at a minimum level but should be designed to meet the needs of each individual student.
2. The Government should consider ring-fencing funds so that support for care leavers in higher education does not have to compete with ordinary placement costs for under-18s.
3. More flexibility should be built into the system to allow young people who are not ready to go to university at 18 to return to higher education with financial support at a later stage.
4. Incentives should be offered to local authorities related to the proportion of formerly looked after children who continue into higher education.
5. Local authorities should be funded to support the education of unaccompanied minors seeking asylum so that all the costs do not fall on a few authorities.
6. Teacher training courses should include a specific module on looked after children.

UCAS

7. The application form should have a box to tick for applicants who are or have been in care, with a note to say that this information will be confidential but will help the HEI to provide any extra resources or information that may be needed.

SCHOOLS

8. Schools should be aware of the educational and support needs of looked after children but also of the risk of underestimating their ability and potential.
9. Before GCSE the Designated Teacher and Year Tutor should have a full discussion with the young person and carer about post-16 plans, including the option of going to university.
10. The pros and cons of remaining at school in Years 12 and 13 as opposed to moving to a further education college should be fully discussed and decisions recorded in the Personal Education Plan and Pathway Plan.
11. The Designated Teacher or Year Head should discuss with the student the advisability of revealing his or her care status when applying for university or college entrance.
12. Schools should recruit university students or graduates willing to act as mentors to disadvantaged young people, and particularly those in care.

LOCAL AUTHORITIES

13. Children in care should be given the chance to attend schools where a high proportion of pupils go on to higher education.
14. Local authorities should plan and budget for increasing numbers of care leavers requiring support through higher education.

15. It should be made clear that being or having been in care is no obstacle to going to university.

16. All young people planning to continue into higher education should be provided with a personal computer or laptop and Internet connection while studying for A levels.

17. Prospective students should be given a copy of the local authority higher education protocol and there should be a written contract detailing the financial and other support on offer based on a full discussion of the student's needs and signed by both parties.

18. Financial support should be sufficient to pay for accommodation and meet basic living costs and educational expenses without forcing the student to take out bank overdrafts or take paid work in term time.

19. Care leavers who go to university should be guaranteed a full after-care service, not contingent on staying within their local authority area. The named Personal Adviser should keep in regular contact throughout their course.

20. The local authority should pay the deposit and hall fees for the first year and rent for a shared house or flat for subsequent years. Students should be strongly advised to live in university accommodation for the first year to reduce travel time and costs and be close to study facilities and social activity.

21. In cases where a young person has been living independently their eligibility for a council tenancy should be guaranteed so that their choice of course and university is not constrained by fear of homelessness.

22. Local authorities should offer holiday grants for long vacations and emphasise the importance of students taking a break before the following academic year.

23. Young people should be formally notified when they are discharged from care, not left to find out by chance.

24. Local authorities should ensure that asylum-seekers who have been in care receive skilled support and advice on status problems and high quality legal representation to enable them to remain in the UK until they have completed their education.

FOSTER CARE

25. Foster care is a key resource for increasing participation of care leavers in higher education. Training for foster carers should be mandatory and include supporting and promoting educational achievement.

26. Some foster carers could be recruited, and paid appropriately, with a specific remit to steer young people through examinations and support them during their time at university.

27. Foster placements should not be ended on the young person's eighteenth birthday. The period between the end of examinations and start of university should be fully funded. Any change of status or placement should be related to the young person's wishes and the educational timetable, not chronological age.

28. Young people should have the option of remaining in their foster homes (or returning to them in vacations) until completion of higher education.

29. Policies on same-race placement should not take precedence over cultural factors, the need for stability or the quality of the relationship between young people and carers.

RESIDENTIAL CARE

30. Local authorities should make much greater use of boarding schools combined with weekend or holiday foster placements as an option for young people in care.

31. Well-motivated young people should never be placed in residential units where the majority of residents are disaffected.

32. All residential homes should provide quiet rooms with study carrels and have an up-to-date reference library. A policy of regular time for homework when no noise is allowed should be enforced. There is a case for providing some residential units for older teenagers with a clear purpose of offering the best possible study conditions for those preparing for examinations.

33. Residents in children's homes should have access to personal computers that are not reserved for staff or locked up after working hours.

34. All children's homes should have a visiting education adviser and arrangements for help with homework if this cannot be provided by existing staff.

35. Young people should be given the option of staying in their home until they have completed post-16 education or training at 18 or 19 and welcomed back in vacations if they go on to higher education. They should not be required to leave until they feel ready for independence.

HEIs

36. All institutions should develop a comprehensive policy relating to young people in or leaving care.

37. All initiatives and publicity aimed at applicants or students from disadvantaged groups should specifically refer to care leavers.

38. More institutions should develop compact arrangements with local authorities to increase participation of care leavers. Universities and colleges running open days and summer schools should ensure that young people in care are specifically invited.

39. Admissions tutors need to understand that it is an exceptional achievement for care leavers to get to the point of applying to university from care and that examination grades may not reflect the young person's potential.

40. Widening participation officers should attend after care workshops and training events on the care system and the needs of care leavers.

41. Care leavers should be given priority for on-campus accommodation and for hardship funds.

42. Student Welfare/Support Services should contact new students known to have been in care and be proactive in offering any necessary help with financial, study or personal problems. They should be alerted to danger signals such as falling behind with assignments.

43. HEIs should ensure that successful applicants who have been in care know before they arrive about any additional grants or bursaries that might be available to them so that they can apply in good time.

References

Bebbington, A. and Miles, J. (1989) 'The background of children who enter local authority care'. *British Journal of Social Work*, 19 (5), 349–68.

Berridge, D. and Brodie, I. (1998) *Children's Homes Revisited*. London: Jessica Kingsley.

Borland, M., Pearson, C., Hill, M., Tisdall, K. and Bloomfield, I. (1998) *Education and Care Away from Home*. Edinburgh: Scottish Council for Research in Education.

Brodie, I. (2003) *Children's Homes and School Exclusion: Redefining the problem*. London: Jessica Kingsley.

Brown, E., Bullock, R., Hobson, C. and Little, M. (1998) *Making Residential Care Work: Structure and culture in children's homes*. Aldershot: Gower.

Children Act 1989 (Chapter 41). London: The Stationery Office.

Children Act 2004 (Chapter 31). London: The Stationery Office.

Children (Leaving Care) Act 2000 (Chapter 35). London: The Stationery Office.

Department for Education and Skills (DfES) (2003a) *Every Child Matters* Online. Available HTTP: <http://www.dfes.gov.uk/pns/DisplayPN.cgi?pnid=20030175> (accessed 18 March 2005).

—— (2003b) *National Statistics Bulletin*. London: DfES.

—— (2003c) *Guidance to the Children (Leaving Care) Act 2000*. London: The Stationery Office.

—— (2003d) *The Future of Higher Education*. London: The Stationery Office.

—— (2004) *National Statistics: Trends in education and skills: 5.5 GCSE/GNVQ Qualifications*. Online. <www.dfes.gov.uk> (accessed 18 March 2005).

—— (2005) *Statistics of Education: Children looked after in England (including adoptions and care leavers) 2003–2004*. London: DfES.

Department of Health (1991a) *The Children Act 1989 Guidance and Regulations Vol. 3 Family Placement*. London: HMSO.

—— (1991b) *The Children Act 1989 Guidance and Regulations Vol. 4 Residential Care*. London: HMSO.

—— (1998) *Quality Protects*. London: Department of Health.

Fletcher-Campbell, F. and Hall, C. (1990) *Changing Schools, Changing People: The education of children in care*. Slough: National Foundation for Educational Research.

Further and Higher Education Act 1992 (Chapter 13). London: The Stationery Office.

Gallagher, B., Brannan, C., Jones, R. and Westwood, S. (2004) 'Good practice in the education of children in residential care'. *British Journal of Social Work*, 34 (8), 1133–60.

Gibbons, J., Conroy, S. and Bell, C. (1995) *Operating the Child Protection System: A study of child protection practices in English local authorities*. London: HMSO.

Harker, R., Dobel-Ober, D., Berridge, D. and Sinclair, R. (2004) *Taking Care of Education: An evaluation of the education of looked after children*. London: National Children's Bureau.

Jackson, S. (1987) *The Education of Children in Care*. Bristol: University of Bristol.

Jackson, S. and Martin, P.Y. (1998) 'Surviving the care system: education and resilience'. *Journal of Adolescence*, 21, 569–83.

Jackson, S. and Roberts, S. (2000) *A Feasibility Study on the Needs of Care Leavers in Higher Education.* Report to the Gulbenkian Foundation. Swansea: University of Wales Swansea School of Social Sciences and International Development.

Jackson, S. and Sachdev, D. (2001) *Better Education, Better Futures: Research, practice and the views of young people in public care.* Ilford: Barnardo's.

Jackson, S. and Thomas, N. (2001) *What Works in Creating Stability for Looked After Children?* Ilford: Barnardo's.

Jackson. S., Ajayi, S. and Quigley, M. (2003) *By Degrees – The First Year: From care to university.* London: National Children's Bureau/Frank Buttle Trust.

Kirby, L. and Fraser, M. (1997) 'Risk and resilience in childhood'. In M. Fraser (ed.), *Risk and Resilience in Childhood: An ecological perspective.* Washington, DC: NASW Press.

Kohli, R. (2000) 'Issues for social work with unaccompanied asylum seeking children'. *Children's Residential Care Unit Newsletter,* 14, 8–10.

Martin, P.Y. and Jackson, S. (2002) 'Educational success for children in public care: advice from a group of high achievers'. *Child and Family Social Work,* 7, 121–30.

Newby, H. (2004) 'Doing widening participation'. Memorial Lecture for Colin Bell, University of Bradford, 30 March 2004.

Pithouse, A., Lowe, K. and Hill-Tout, J. (2004) 'Foster carers who care for children with challenging behaviour: a total population study'. *Adoption & Fostering,* 28 (3), 20–30.

Social Exclusion Unit (SEU) (2003) *A Better Education for Children in Care.* London: SEU.

Social Services Inspectorate (SSI) and Ofsted (1995) *The Education of Children who are Looked After by Local Authorities.* London: Department of Health/Ofsted.

Triseliotis, J., Borland, M., Hill, M. and Lambert, L. (1995) *Teenagers and the Social Work Service.* London: HMSO.

Triseliotis, J., Borland, M. and Hill, M. (2000) *Delivering Foster Care.* London: British Agencies for Adoption and Fostering.

US Department of Labor (2000) *Standard Occupational Classification.* Washington, DC: Bureau of Labor Statistics.

Utting, W. (1991) *Children in the Public Care: A review of residential care.* London: HMSO.

Utting, W. (1997) People Like Us: The report of the review of the safeguards for children living away from home. London: The Stationery Office.

Who Cares? Trust (2004) *Measuring Progress: Enabling children in care to fulfil their educational potential.* London: The Who Cares? Trust.

Appendix 1
The path from care to graduation

SUMMARY OF RECOMMENDATIONS FROM THE INTERIM REPORT

PREPARING THE GROUND

- All children in care should be looked after in an environment in which education is valued, encouraged and supported.
- The idea that university is a desirable and attainable goal should be planted as early as possible.
- They should be assured of the maximum possible stability in their home circumstances, particularly during examination periods and the weeks and months leading up to them.
- From the moment that students embark on A-level or equivalent courses they should be provided with full information on degree courses and universities to which they might later apply.
- They should be encouraged and funded to take full advantage of summer schools and open days provided by universities and colleges.
- Young people from overseas need special consideration and support.

APPLYING TO UNIVERSITY

- From the end of Year 12 prospective students should be helped to shape outline plans. For instance, should they go away to university or choose a course near home?
- At this stage the student needs a firm assurance of financial support and an explanation of how this will be calculated.
- Expert help should be provided to assist with completion of the UCAS application form.
- Young people should be given an opportunity to discuss their choice of university and course with a well-informed person, if necessary on several occasions.
- If called for interview they should be given help to prepare themselves and all travelling expenses should be paid, including those of a companion if they feel it necessary for someone to go with them.
- On the day that examination results are received an appropriate person should be available to check if conditional offers have been met, and if not to offer comfort and decide what action might be taken.

ACCOMMODATION AND MONEY

These are factors that can cause problems for any student, but far more so for those who lack family support.

- The student should be given help in making plans for living accommodation, both at university and during vacations. Local authorities need to be aware that hall fees and living costs differ dramatically between institutions.
- Students should be able to return to former foster families or retain existing tenancies to provide stability at least through their first year.
- The local authority should ensure that each young person begins his or her university course with appropriate clothing and equipment, including an up-to-date computer.

- They should be given detailed assistance with budgeting both before and during their course if necessary.
- Financial support should be adapted to the specific needs of individual students. It should be at a level that does not require them to work during term time and should be reassessed each year.

SUPPORT FROM THE CORPORATE PARENT

- The local authority should ensure that a known person accompanies the student to university at the start of the year to provide transport and help with settling in.
- The local authority should have a clear policy on help for those who get into financial difficulties, especially when, for whatever reason, they are unable to meet basic needs.
- A designated representative of the local authority must keep in regular touch with the student and not rely on them to make contact.
- This person should keep track of the student's performance in end-of-year assessments and examinations and give encouragement and support as appropriate.

CELEBRATING SUCCESS

- The local authority should be proud of the young person's achievement and mark it by ensuring that someone of the student's choice can attend the degree ceremony. The usual expenses should be met, including travel costs, hire of academic dress, photographs and a celebratory meal.

Appendix 2
By Degrees *Advisory Group*

Sir William Utting (Chair)
Professor Peter Aggleton (Institute of Education, University of London)
Mark Burrows (Department of Health)
Laura Chapman (Freemasons' Grand Charity)
Susanna Cheal (The Who Cares? Trust)
Jo Collins (KPMG Foundation)
Dr Geoffrey Copland (Universities UK)
Neil Flint (Department for Education and Skills)
Hilary Hodgson (Esmée Fairbairn Foundation)
Dr Peter McParlin (North Yorkshire County Council)
Dr Gillian Pugh (Coram Family)
Dr Ruth Sinclair (National Children's Bureau)

Hugo Perks (Director, Frank Buttle Trust) from 2001–2003
Gerri McAndrew (Chief Executive, Frank Buttle Trust) from September 2003
Sarah Lawley (Frank Buttle Trust)
Karen Melton (Frank Buttle Trust)
Christine Manning-Prior (Frank Buttle Trust)

Professor Sonia Jackson (Research Director)
Sarah Ajayi (Research Officer)
Margaret Quigley (Research Officer)

Appendix 3
Universities and colleges attended by participants

By Degrees students studied at 68 different higher education institutions. Where more than one participant attended a particular institution the number of attendees is given in brackets.

University of Bath
University of Birmingham
Bolton Institute
Bournemouth University (3)
Bradford University (2)
Brighton University (3)
Brunel University (6)
Buckinghamshire Chilterns University College
University of Central England
Chester College of Higher Education
Christ Church College, Canterbury
City University
Coventry University
Dearne Valley College, Doncaster
De Montfort University (2)
University of Derby
University of Durham
University of East Anglia (3)
University of East London
Edinburgh University
Essex University
University of Gloucestershire (2)
Goldsmiths College
University of Greenwich
Hartford College, Cheshire
University of Huddersfield
University of Hull
University of Kent (3)
King Alfred's College, Winchester
Kingston University (4)
Leeds College of Art and Design
University of Leeds
University of Liverpool
Liverpool John Moores University (2)
London University School of Oriental and African Studies
London Guildhall University
London Metropolitan University (4)

London South Bank University (5)
University College London
London College of Printing (2)
Manchester Metropolitan University (9)
Middlesex University
University of Manchester
Nottingham Trent University
University of Nottingham
University College, Northampton (3)
University of Oxford
Oxford Brookes University
Plymouth University (2)
Queen Mary College (3)
Reaseheath College
Roehampton University
Royal Holloway College
Sheffield Hallam University (4)
St Mary's College
Staffordshire University
Stoke on Trent University
Sunderland University
Surrey Institute of Art and Design (2)
University of Salford
University of Southampton
University of Surrey (2)
University of Sussex (3)
Thames Valley University (4)
Warwickshire College, Royal Leamington Spa
University of the West of England (2)
Westminster University (5)
West Thames College (2)

Appendix 4

Publications and presentations by the By Degrees *research team 2001–2004*

PUBLICATIONS

Ajayi, S. and Jackson, S. (2002) 'University challenge'. *Community Care*, 19 September, 44–5.

Ajayi, S. and Quigley, M. (2003) 'Care leavers entering higher education: the provision of financial and personal support'. *ChildRIGHT*, July/August, 9–11.

Cox, P. and Jackson, S. (2003) *Researching Social Work*. Themed Issue of *Social Work Education*, 22 (1), February 2003.

Jackson, S. (2002) 'Promoting stability and continuity in care away from home'. In D. McNeish, T. Newman and H. Roberts (eds), *What Works for Children?* Buckingham: Open University Press.

Jackson, S. and Ajayi, S. (2002) *By Degrees – From Care to University: Emerging findings from the first year of the study*. A report to the Social Exclusion Unit. London: Thomas Coram Research Unit, Institute of Education.

Jackson, S., Ajayi, S. and Quigley, M. (2002) *Care Leavers in Higher Education: What progress has been made in implementing the Children (Leaving Care) Act 2000?* A report to the Social Exclusion Unit. London: Thomas Coram Research Unit, Institute of Education.

Jackson, S., Feinstein, L., Levacic, R., Owen, C., Simon, A. and Brassett-Grundy, A. (2002) *The Costs and Benefits of Educating Children in Care. CLS Cohort Studies Working Paper No. 4*. Based upon a report to the Social Exclusion Unit from the Thomas Coram Research Unit.

Jackson, S., Ajayi, S. and Quigley, M. (2003) *By Degrees – The First Year: From care to university*. London: National Children's Bureau/Frank Buttle Trust. (ISBN 1 900990 93 8) (The Interim Report)

Martin, P.Y. and Jackson, S. (2002) 'Educational success for children in public care: advice from a group of high achievers'. *Child and Family Social Work*, 7 (2), 121–30.

Mittler, P. and Jackson, S. (2002) 'Social exclusion and education'. *MCC: Building Knowledge for Integrated Care*, 10 (3), 5–13.

PRESENTATIONS (IN DATE ORDER)

Research team members have spoken at 44 conferences and workshops since the start of the *By Degrees* project.

Jackson, S. (2001) '*By Degrees*'. Keynote speech and workshop at interprofessional conference *Tools for the Job: Intervention techniques to encourage and celebrate success*, Coventry City Council, January.

Jackson, S. (2001) 'Promoting continuity and success in education'. *Research in Practice Symposium*, Manchester, January.

Jackson, S. (2001) 'What the research tells us'. *Creating Opportunities for the Education of Children in Public Care*, Hertfordshire County Council Conference, Hatfield, March.

Jackson, S. (2001) 'Raising the educational achievement of children in public care'. Joint seminar, Wiltshire County Council and University of Bath, April.

Jackson, S. (2001) 'Nobody ever told us school mattered'. Chair's address, British Agencies for Adoption and Fostering (BAAF) and National Teaching and Advisory Service Conferences, Liverpool and London, May.

Jackson, S. (2001) Keynote speeches to launch the Barnardo's publication *Better Education, Better Futures*. Conferences in Edinburgh, Belfast, Cardiff, Llandudno, May.

Jackson, S. (2001) 'The path from care to prison'. Paper presented at Howard League for Penal Reform Annual Conference, University College, Oxford, September.

Jackson, S. (2001) 'Creating stability for children in care'. University of Queensland, Cairns, Australia, October.

Jackson, S. (2001) 'Promoting resilience'. Invited seminar for Ian Potter Foundation, Melbourne, Australia, October.

Jackson, S. (2001) 'Raising the educational attainment of children in care: research and progress in the UK'. Keynote presentation at Uniting Care Burnside Conference, *Making the Grade*, Paramatta, NSW, October.

Jackson, S. (2001) 'The importance of education for children in out-of-home care'. Macquarie Lecture at Parliament House, Sydney, Australia, October.

Jackson, S. (2001) 'Social exclusion and the miseducation of children in care'. Presentation at Centre for Social Policy Fellows Meeting, Dartington Hall, November.

Jackson, S, and Ajayi, S. (2001) *By Degrees* research presented at the *By Degrees* launch. London Voluntary Sector Resource Centre, December.

Jackson, S. (2002) 'The education of looked after children'. Seminar at the School for Policy Studies, University of Bristol, March.

Jackson, S. (2002) '*By Degrees* research'. Seminar for the Department of Social Work, University of Edinburgh, April.

Jackson, S. (2002) 'Raising the attainment of looked after children'. National Assembly for Wales Conference *Caring for the Education of Looked After Children in Wales*, Llandrindod Wells, May.

Jackson, S. (2002) Keynote address, Denbighshire County Council Annual Head Teacher Conference, St Asaph, October.

Jackson, S. (2002) 'The interaction between education and mental health'. Association of Child Psychologists and Psychiatrists, Leicester, October.

Jackson, S. (2002)'Putting education at the centre'. Herefordshire County Council Conference *Firm Foundations for a Better Future*, Hereford, November.

Jackson, S. (2003) 'Care leavers in higher education'. *Education Matters* Seminar, The Who Cares? Trust, Commonwealth Club, London, January.

Jackson, S. (2003)'Improving life chances for children: current research'. Cornwall County Council Joint Agency Conference, Newquay, February.

Jackson, S. (2003) 'Better education, better futures – what research has to tell us'. Wrexham County Council Conference *Education Matters*, North East Wales Institute, Wrexham, February.

Jackson, S. (2003) 'Late foster placements – a second chance for stability and educational success'. Paper presented at the Nuffield Foundation National Seminar on Stability in Fostercare, Royal Academy of Engineering, Westminster, February.

Quigley, M. (2003) *By Degrees* research presented at *Wanted – A Helping Hand: easing the transition of socially isolated groups into tertiary education* organised by SNAP (Scottish Network for Access and Participation) in Inverness, Scotland, March.

Ajayi, S., Jackson, S. and Quigley, M. (2003) '*By Degrees*: The first year. From Care to University'. Interim report presented at the *By Degrees* Conference organised by the National Children's Bureau, London, May.

Jackson, S. (2003) 'Children and their potential'. Swindon interprofessional conference *Give Us a Chance*, Bath, June.

Ajayi, S., Perks, H. and Quigley, M. (2003) *By Degrees* research presented at the *Quality Protects* Leaving Care Project Team Meeting organised by the Department of Health, London, July.

Ajayi, S. (2003) *By Degrees* research presented in a workshop at the Wales Leaving Care Forum organised by the Welsh Assembly Government. Aberystwyth, Wales. September.

Jackson, S. (2003) 'The role of education in promoting resilience'. Wiltshire Children and Young People's Services Partnership, Devizes, September.

Quigley, M. (2003) *By Degrees* research presented at the North West Aftercare Forum, St Helens, October.

Quigley, M. and Ajayi, S. (2003) *By Degrees* research presented for the *Quality Protects* Conference *Good Enough For Our Children – Is Corporate Parenting Working?*, London, November.

Jackson, S. (2003) 'Smart future – a better education for children in care'. Social Exclusion Unit/DfES Conference, London, December.

Jackson, S. (2003) '*By Degrees* – from care to university', South West Leaving Care Forum, Taunton Vale, December.

Jackson, S., Ajayi, S. and Quigley, M. (2004) *By Degrees* research presented at DFES Conference, *Supporting Young People Leaving Care to Achieve in Higher Education*, Institute of Education, London, January.

Ajayi, S. and Quigley, M. (2004) 'University not McDonalds – raising the aspirations of care leavers'. *By Degrees* research presented at the Institute of Education Open Day, February.

Jackson, S. (2004) 'No Ceiling – going to university from care'. National Children's Bureau Conference *Leaving Care*, London, February.

Jackson, S., Ajayi, S. and Quigley, M. (2004) 'Encouraging young people in care into higher education'. National Children's Bureau Conference *Taking Care of Education – Evaluating the education of children in care*, London, March.

Jackson, S. (2004) 'Aiming higher'. Keynote address at the Conwy County Borough Council Conference, North Wales Conference Centre, Llandudno, May.

Jackson, S. (2004) 'The role of education in promoting resilience and recovery from trauma'. Invited lecture at the International University Centre, Dubrovnik, June.

Jackson, S. (2004) 'Educational outcomes for children in public care: what research tells us'. Keynote address at Conference on the *Education of Looked After Children: Everybody's business*, Islington Borough Council, June.

(S. Jackson presented prizes and spoke about *By Degrees* at Hampshire Social Services Award Ceremony for children and young people in care, Marwell Zoo Hotel, Winchester, July 2004.)

Jackson, S. (2004) 'Aiming higher'. Keynote address at the Tameside Borough Council Conference on Education of Children in Care, Dukinfield, October.

Jackson, S. (2004) 'Creating stability for young people in care'. Invited paper presented at the Nordic Campbell Collaboration Conference, Copenhagen, November.

Jackson, S. (2004) 'Resilience'. Keynote address for the Educational Psychologists Services in the South of England, Sandbanks Hotel, Poole, December.

McAndrew, G. (2004) '*By Degrees*: the first year – action research project tracking care leavers into higher education'. Presentation at the Aim Higher Conference, Leicester, December.

Appendix 5

Financial support for care leavers at university

THE FRANK BUTTLE TRUST BENCHMARK FIGURES 2004/05

The benchmark figures shown in the table are used as a basis for the Frank Buttle Trust to calculate grant aid for students in higher education. In the final interview all participants were asked to comment on these figures. Most respondents stressed the need for funding to be adapted to circumstances, such as geographical location and the type of course that the student was taking. Of those interviewed 92 per cent considered that the figures would provide adequate financial support for a young person from care on a university course. The remainder suggested minor adjustments.

These guidelines are interpreted flexibly and are always related to individual circumstances and requirements.

The National Union of Students estimated that the average student expenditure for 2003/04 was £193 per week for those living in London and £164 per week for those outside.

	London		Outside London	
	2003/04	2004/05	2003/04	2004/05
	£	£	£	£
Rent	77.00	78.54	62.00	63.24
Lighting/heating	10.00	10.20	10.00	10.20
Food	32.00	32.64	32.00	32.64
Travel	15.00	15.30	12.00	12.24
Clothing	7.00	7.14	7.00	7.14
Laundry	5.00	5.10	5.00	5.10
Books and equipment	9.00	9.18	9.00	9.18
Personal hygiene	6.00	6.12	6.00	6.12
Insurance	2.00	2.04	2.00	2.04
Discretionary	25.00	25.50	23.00	23.46
Total per week	**188.00**	**191.76**	**168.00**	**171.36**
Total academic year 38 weeks	**7144.00**	**7286.88**	**6384.00**	**6511.68**
Student loan	4930.00	5050.00	4000.00	4095.00
Difference	**−2214.00**	**−2236.88**	**−2384.00**	**−2416.68**

NB: The deficits for 2004/05 could be reduced by £1000 if applicants qualify for the full Higher Education Grant or more if living in Wales or Scotland.

VARIATIONS IN DISCRETIONARY SPENDING

	Living at home		Living in shared accommodation (hostel, shared house etc.)		Living alone in own accommodation	
	2003/04	2004/05	2003/04	2004/05	2003/04	2004/05
	£	£	£	£	£	£
London	15.00	15.30	20.00	20.40	25.00	25.50
Outside London	13.00	13.26	18.00	18.36	23.00	23.46

BOOKS AND EQUIPMENT

Minimum of £9 per week for those on academic courses, maximum of £15 per week for practical courses and the more expensive degree courses. Higher amounts considered where evidence provided suggests the maximum figure needs to be exceeded.

Index